Robinson R22
A Pilot's Guide

John Swan

ISBN 1 874783 31 4

Airplan Flight Equipment
1a Ringway Trading Estate
Shadowmoss Road
Manchester M22 5LH
Tel: 0161 499 0023
Fax: 0161 499 0298
www.afeonline.com

First Edition 2001

©Copyright 2001 John Swan and AFE Ltd.

Re-printed with amendments 2002

Printed in the United States of America

Robinson R22
A Pilot's Guide
John Swan

ISBN 1 874783 31 4

Airplan Flight Equipment
1a Ringway Trading Estate
Shadowmoss Road
Manchester M22 5LH
Tel: 0161 499 0023
Fax: 0161 499 0298
www.afeonline.com

Contents

Section 6   Loading and Performance

Section 7   Awareness Training

Section 8   Conversions

Index

Authors Acknowledgments

I would like to thank all those whose knowledge, help and advice went into this book, in particular:

Chris Alan

Cherry Bowier

Stan Bowier

CAA Safety Promotion Section

Sandra Kavanagh

Vicky Leonard

Sloane Helicopters Ltd

Westair Aviation Ltd

Publishers Acknowledgments

Edited by Louise Southern with special thanks to the following contributors:

Burman Aviation

Jeff Hards

Heliair Ltd

Mike Smith

Allan Ramsden

Rob Taylor (gdi-studio.co.uk)

Kurt Robinson

Robinson Helicopter Company

Tiger Helicopters Ltd

Section 1
General Description

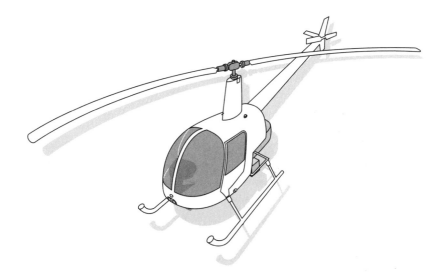

The Robinson R22

With the introduction of the R22 helicopter in 1979, the light piston-engine helicopter market was revolutionised.

Originally envisaged as a low cost personal helicopter for the average family, its role soon changed and expanded into the fields of radio and television reporting, site support, aerial photography and filming, airborne law enforcement, personal and business transport, cattle herding and flight training.

This book covers all R22s from the standard through HP, Alpha, Beta and Mariner, to the Beta II and Mariner II. The R22 Beta II and Mariner II are powered by the Lycoming 0-360 series engine, whereas all other R22s are powered by the Lycoming O-320 series engine, both engines being de-rated to 124BHP for continuous use.

With the introduction of the Alpha and Beta models an auxiliary fuel tank was added increasing the range and endurance by 50%. To retain similar cabin weights with this increased fuel load, the gross weight was also increased by 70lbs to 1370lbs.

The Mariner and Mariner II, the float equipped R22s, permit extended flight over water, allowing the possibility of landing on remote lakes.

Production has passed the 3,000 mark, with over 35% of UK registered helicopters being R22s. Robinson launched their R44, four seater to the European market in 1997, production has now exceeded 950.

R22

PILOT'S OPERATING HANDBOOK

AND FAA APPROVED
ROTORCRAFT FLIGHT MANUAL

RTR 061

FAA APPROVED IN NORMAL CATEGORY BASED ON FAR 27 AND FAR 21. THIS HANDBOOK INCLUDES THE MATERIAL REQUIRED TO BE FURNISHED TO THE PILOT BY FAR 27 AND FAR 21 AND MUST BE CARRIED IN THE HELICOPTER AT ALL TIMES.

HELICOPTER SERIAL NO. _EI-XMA   0681_

HELICOPTER REGISTRATION NO. _EI-XMA_

SECTIONS 2, 3, 4 AND 5
FAA APPROVED BY: _Donald Armstrong_

CHIEF, FLIGHT TEST SECTION
ENGINEERING AND MANUFACTURING BRANCH
FEDERAL AVIATION ADMINISTRATION, WESTERN REGION

DATE: _Mar. 16, 1979_

ROBINSON HELICOPTER CO.
TORRANCE, CALIFORNIA

The approved Pilot Operating Handbook/Flight Manual (illustrated above), as amended, is the only source of authoritative information. Each individual aircraft has its own individual POH/FM, in the interests of safety & good airmanship the pilot should be familiar with this document.

Model and Production Years

R22

1979-1983	R22 standard	1985-1996	R22 Mariner
1979-present	R22 HP	1996-present	R22 Beta II
1983-present	R22 Alpha	1996-present	R22 Mariner II
1985-1996	R22 Beta		

R22 Beta

R22 Beta II

R22 Mariner

R22 HP

The Airframe

The R22 airframe is of all metal construction, the primary fuselage structure is of welded steel tubing and riveted aluminium panels, the tailcone is an aluminium monocoque, with the skins carrying the primary loads. Some non-structural components, such as doors, ducts, fairings and secondary cabin structures are manufactured from fibreglass and thermoplastic. Stainless steel firewalls

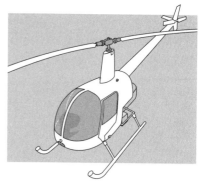

are located forward and above the engine compartment. The helicopter is fitted with skid type landing gear.

To enhance the stability of the R22 in the cruise a vertical and horizontal stabiliser are fitted to the rear of the tail cone.

A cowl door on the pilot's side of the helicopter allows access to the main rotor gear box and the drive train. Several removable panels give access to controls and other components, for maintenance purposes. The instrument console hinges up to allow access to the instruments, wiring and in the case of the Standard, HP and Mariner models, the battery.

The Flying Controls

Although at first glance the T bar cyclic looks rather different from the conventional cyclic, it works in exactly the same manner. The R22 is fitted with dual controls as standard, detachable duals are an option. All primary controls use push/pull tubes and bell cranks, only sealed ball bearings or self lubricated teflon rod ends are used, this helps to keep routine maintenance to a minimum.

The non conventional cyclic stick, note the position of the black thumb turn at the base of the cyclic, this is the cyclic friction.

The function of the cyclic stick is to tilt the main rotor disc in the direction of desired movement of the helicopter, so a forward movement of the cyclic tilts the rotor disc forward, resulting in the helicopter moving forward. To make the helicopter turn, the cyclic is moved laterally, resulting in the helicopter banking and turning as an aeroplane does.

The collective stick, or lever, is of conventional design with a twist grip throttle and governer switch on the end. A raising of the collective increases the pitch evenly on all main rotor blades, causing them to generate more lift.

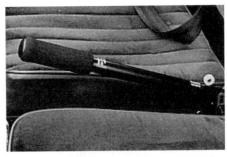

The conventional collective, note the friction is off, the white wheel above the collective being forward.

The governor maintains RPM constant through all phases of powered flight. Its sensors feed signals to one servo motor on the throttle, which makes appropriate movements when the engine RPM start to deviate.

The pedals are also of conventional design, controlling the thrust generated by the tail rotor. The prime function of the tail rotor is to counteract the torque of the main rotor and hence stop the fuselage spinning in the opposite direction. Varying the thrust generated by the tail rotor allows the helicopter to be rotated in either direction when hovering.

The collective and cyclic are both fitted with frictions and trims, the frictions are solely for use on the ground, they hold the controls in position and allow the pilot to use both hands for the start up and shut down procedures. The collective trim balances the feedback forces from the main rotor and allows the pilot to remove his left hand from the collective in cruise flight, for example to change radio frequencies or check flight plan details. Note, the pilot should keep his left hand on the collective when ever possible in case of engine failure which requires an immediate lowering of the collective, any delay could be fatal. The collective trim can only be adjusted by a licensed engineer. The cyclic has a fixed fore and aft trim which tends to balance out the stick forces in this plane in the cruise. A lateral trim is fitted, it is either on or off (pulled up or pushed in respectively), on R22s from serial number 550 onwards it is adjustable. When the cyclic trim knob is pulled up, on, it off-loads the high forces tending to push the cyclic to the left in cruise. Note that at slow speed, other aerodynamic factors predominate, and this effect is not felt, hence the trim knob is pushed in for slow flight or hovering manoeuvres.

The cyclic trim is shown pulled up, the normal position for cruise.

> ## CAUTION
>
> On certain R22s the cyclic trim knob is located next to the mixture control. To pull the trim on the pilot must reach around the cyclic, this will prevent the possibility of inadvertently pulling the mixture and therefore stopping the engine in flight.

Detachable controls on the passenger side are an option. The pedals are removed by pulling the tab on each pedal upright, back, twisting each pedal anti-clockwise and pulling the pedal up and away from the floor. The reverse is applicable for their installation.

The cyclic stick splits just to the left of the T-bar teetering hinge. The locking pin is removed by pushing the button in, while pulling the pin out. The cyclic can then be pulled off to the left: place the protective plastic cap over the exposed cyclic tube to prevent possible injury. Also place the lock pin into the detached cyclic to prevent misplacing the lock pin. Reinstallation of the left cyclic is the opposite of removal: place the protective plastic cap under the seat to prevent loss.

The collective lever/twist grip throttle is removed by untieing and opening the leather cover at the base of the passenger collective. This reveals the two locking pins, which when pushed in allow the whole collective/throttle to be pulled away. Installation is the reverse, ensure that the placard on the collective is facing up and both locking pins are fully engaged through both holes on the collective. To aid location of the spring clip, gently rotate the collective either way until the two pins pop home. Finally, check the twist grip throttle operation to ensure movement of the passenger's throttle moves the pilot's throttle.

The Landing Gear

The skid landing gear is of the spring and yield type, relying on elastic flexing of two cross tubes to absorb any landing shocks. An extremely heavy landing will cause the centre cross tube to yield, the four struts will tend to hinge up and out. Slight yielding of the cross

The simple skid landing gear.

tubes is approved. However, if yielding is severe enough to place the tail skid within three feet (two feet for standard and HP's) of the ground when sitting empty, the cross tube must be replaced.

To prevent wear to the skids due to run on landings, skid shoes are located at three points on the underside of each skid. These should be replaced when their thinnest point is less than $\frac{1}{16}$ inch.

The Engine

The R22s are all fitted with the Avco Lycoming O-320/0-360 series of engine. The standard R22 uses the O-320-A2B or A2C engine generating a maximum of 150BHP at 2700RPM. The R22 HP, Beta and Mariner are fitted with the O-320-B2C engine generating a maximum of 160BHP at 2700RPM. The R22 Beta II and Mariner II use the 0-360-J2A engine generating a maximum of 180BHP at 2700RPM. In all cases to ensure engine and transmission lives of 2000 hours between major overhauls, the engines are derated to a continuous rating of 124BHP at 2652RPM (104% Rotor RPM).

In the Beta, Beta II, Mariner and Mariner II application there is a five minute take-off rating of 131BHP at 2652RPM.

The engine is a four cylinder unit with cylinders horizontally opposed across the crankshaft. The cylinders are staggered so that each connecting rod has its own crankshaft throw. The cylinders and crank case assembly are manufactured from aluminium alloy castings.

The 0-320 engine installation, the squirrel cage cooling fan is to the rear of the engine just below the tail boom.

The engine is air cooled, a large direct drive squirrel cage cooling fan at the rear of the helicopter engine bay forces cooling air through a shroud to the top of the engine. Baffles guide this air down around the deeply finned cylinders, these fins increase the surface area of the cylinders in contact with the air and aid cooling. Air is also bled from the top of the engine and supplied as cooling air to the alternator, the main gearbox and the oil cooler.

The engine is mounted in the steel tubular section of the helicopter below the main gearbox by four large rubber mounts just aft of the firewall.

The Drive System

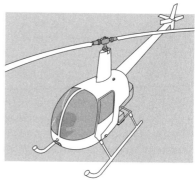

Power is taken from the output shaft of the engine, at the rear of the engine bay, by two double V-belts up to the upper pulley (upper sheave). The clutch actuator moves the upper pulley upwards to tension the V-belts; on start up the V-belts are slack and slip, enabling the engine to start under no load. The upper pulley has a larger diameter than the lower, giving a speed reduction of 0.8536:1, it also contains the freewheel unit, sprag clutch, which allows the main and tail rotors to continue rotating (autorotate) if the engine stops. The inner shaft of the freewheel unit transmits power forward to the main rotor gearbox, and up to the main rotor, and aft via the tail rotor drive shaft and gearbox to the tail rotor. Flexible couplings at the input to the main rotor gearbox and at either end of the long tail rotor drive shaft allow for any slight misalignments in the drive train.

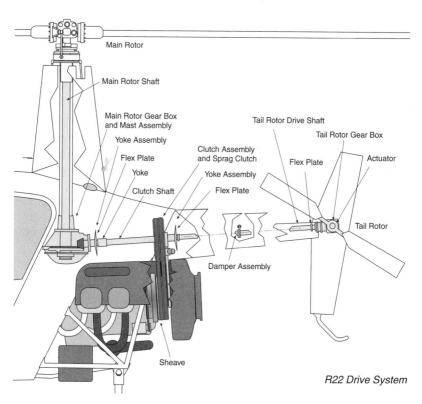

R22 Drive System

The main rotor gearbox contains a single stage spiral bevel gear set, with a reduction ratio of 11:47, which is splash lubricated. Cooling air is fed via a duct from the top of the engine to the bottom of the gearbox casing. The gearbox is mounted to the steel tubular fuselage by four large rubber mounts.

The long tail rotor drive shaft has no bearings supporting it but has a lightly loaded damper, located just forward of its midpoint. The tail rotor gearbox contains a spiral bevel gear set, with a speed increase of 3:2, which is splash lubricated. The input and the output shafts of the tail rotor gearbox are manufactured from stainless steel, all other shafts are manufactured of alloy steel and hence subject to corrosion.

The Clutch Actuator

Once the engine is started the double V belts are tensioned by the clutch actuator raising the upper pulley. The clutch actuator is located between the upper and lower pulleys, selecting "engage" on the clutch switch raises the upper pulley and tensions the belts. A sensor in the actuator measures the V belt tension and switches off the actuator when the V belts are correctly tensioned. This is indicated to the pilot by the orange clutch warning light going out. When the clutch light

The clutch actuator motor is just visible above the cooling fan shroud.

is on the V belts are either tensioning or untensioning or if the belts are worn, the over travel micro switch has tripped in. Selecting "disengage" lowers the upper pulley and untensions the belts, when the V belts are fully untensioned the clutch warning light also goes out. A separate low amperage fuse, located on the steel tubing just forward of the upper pulley, stops a motor overload tripping the circuit breaker and prematurely turning off the clutch warning light.

The Tachometers

The R22 is equipped with a dual tachometer for the engine and rotor RPM's. Although these dual electronic tachometers are not of the conventional concentric type, they are easy to read. The engine tachometer is driven from one of the magnetos while the rotor tachometer picks up its signals from the two magnets rotating on the main gearbox flexible coupling. Each tachometer is completely independent from the other, they both have their own circuit breaker. Both have power supplied from the alternator, and directly from the battery even when the master battery switch is turned off. Only if the clutch switch is also selected to disengage, or the battery goes totally flat, will the power to the tachometers cease.

> ## CAUTION
>
> The unapproved installation of electrical devices can effect the accuracy and reliability of the electronic tachometers, approval must come from Robinson.

The non conventional dual tachometer is the top right hand instrument.

The Rotor Systems

The main rotor has a diameter of 25' 2", and comprises of two all metal blades with a chord of 7" and a washout (twist) of 8°, mounted to the hub by individual coning hinges. The hub is connected to the main rotor shaft by a teeter hinge located above the two coning hinges, it is therefore an underslung rotor system. The main rotor blades consist of a D shaped stainless steel leading

The main rotor hub showing the central teetering hinge above the two coning hinges.

edge spar, an aluminium honeycomb filler and aluminium skins, the thick stainless steel leading edge resists corrosion and erosion due to dust particles, sand and rain.

Stainless steel
leading edge

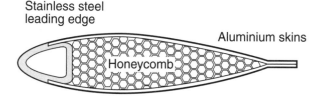

Aluminium skins

Honeycomb

R22 Main Rotor Blade

The pitch change bearings are located in a housing in the root of each blade, the housing is filled with oil and hermetically sealed with a neoprene boot. The coning, teetering hinges and the pitch link rod ends are all self lubricating teflon bearings.

The flapping restraint mechanism for the main rotor blades come into effect as the rotor slows, and due to the reduction in centrifugal force the blades pivot down about their respective coning hinges. This produces a friction restraint about the teetering hinge preventing the rotor from see-sawing while stopping or starting the rotors.

The tail rotor has a diameter of 3' 6", a chord of 4" and has a fixed coning angle, it consists of two all metal blades mounted on an offset teetering hub (delta hinge). The tail rotor blades are constructed from aluminium honeycombed spars and forged aluminium

The R22 tail rotor.

root fittings with wrap around aluminium skins. The bellcrank, offset teetering and pitch change bearings have self lubricating teflon liners.

The Ignition System

The engine features a dual ignition system, fitted with two magnetos. The magnetos are small electrical AC generators which are driven by the crankshaft rotation to provide a very high voltage to a distributor, which directs it via high voltage leads (or high tension leads) to the spark plugs. At the spark plug the current must cross a gap, in doing so a spark is produced which ignites the fuel/air mixture in the cylinder.

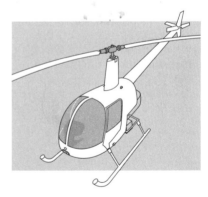

The magnetos are fitted at the rear of the engine, one on each side of the engine centre line (hence Left and Right magnetos). Note. The engine is installed backwards in the R22, hence the magnetos are at the front of the engine bay. The standard arrangement is for each magneto to fire one of the

Front of helicopter

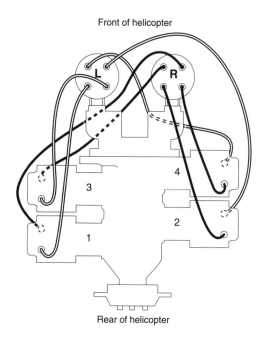

Rear of helicopter

two spark plugs in each cylinder, each cylinder has two spark plugs (top and bottom) for safety and efficiency. The leads that run from the magnetos to the spark plugs should be secure and there should be no splits or cracks in the plastic insulation covering the leads.

It is worth emphasising that the ignition system is totally independent of the helicopter electrical system, and once the engine is running it will operate regardless of the serviceability of the battery or alternator.

The Oil System

The oil system of the engine provides for lubrication, cooling, sealing, cleansing and protection against corrosion. The system is a wet sump, pressure feed system. The oil sump is located under the engine, and oil is drawn from there, through a filter screen by the engine driven oil pump and to a bypass valve. This valve routes the oil to the oil cooler when the oil is hot, from there the oil passes through a pressure relief valve, and then into the oil gallery of the crankshaft. When the oil has flowed around the engine it drains down to the sump by gravity. The function of the pressure relief valve is to regulate the oil pressure over a wide range of temperatures and power settings. In the case of high oil pressure the valve allows oil to return to the sump without going into the engine.

Oil contents can be checked on a dipstick which is accessible from the front of the engine bay on the co pilot's side between the forward cylinder and the firewall. The dipstick is graduated in US quarts and measures the contents of the oil sump. When the engine has been running, the oil may take up to 10 minutes to return to the sump, only then can a true reading be taken. When replacing the dipstick care should be taken not to overtighten the cap. To do so can make it exceptionally difficult to open the cap again, and it is quite possible to strip the thread on the filler pipe.

The oil filler pipe is located forward of the engine on the co pilot's side.

The oil temperature gauge mounted in the cockpit is electrically operated and measures temperature from a sender unit in the engine, a separate pressure sender unit and electrical circuit is connected to the low oil pressure warning light.

The Starter System

The starter motor is attached to the engine at the rear of the engine bay on the pilot's side. It incorporates a geared cog that engages on to the teeth of the starter ring gear when the magneto key switch is turned to START. With the magneto key in the START position a vibrator is energised and supplies a shower of sparks to a set of starter points in the magneto, this retards the spark and aids starting. When the engine fires and begins to rotate under its own power the magneto key switch is released, allowing it to return to the BOTH position, the cog on the starter motor withdraws to be clear of the starter ring gear, and the starter vibrator is de-energised.

On certain models, a STARTER WARNING LIGHT is fitted in the cockpit. This illuminates when the starter is operated to show the starter motor is engaging the starter ring gear. When the magneto key switch is released the light should go out. If the light remains on this means that the starter motor is still engaged to the starter ring gear. In this instance the starter motor is being turned by the engine, and serious damage may be caused to the aircraft electrical system. In this case the engine should be shut down without delay.

When fitted, the starter warning light is located in the centre of the warning lights along the top of the instrument panel.

The Fuel System

The fuel system is a gravity feed system and hence requires no fuel pumps. The main fuel tank has a usable capacity of 19.2 US gallons and the auxiliary fuel tank, fitted to the Alpha and Beta models, has a usable capacity of 10.5 US gallons. Two panel mounted fuel gauges are electrically operated by float type transmitters in each tank, E indicates no usable fuel left, the main tank has a separate electrical sensor which

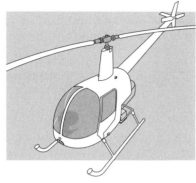

activates the low fuel warning light when approximately 1 US gallon of fuel remains. A dip stick is supplied to visually check the fuel quantity in each tank. Both fuel tanks are vented through the mast fairing. There are three fuel drains, one on each fuel tank and one on the gascolator, fuel filter. To drain the main tank an extended plastic tube, just aft of the passengers door, is pushed in and the sample collected in a plastic container. The auxiliary tank's drain is accessible from inside the cowling door, pressing up the plastic tube will drain fuel from the outer tube at the bottom of firewall on the pilot's side. The gascolator is found on the bottom of the firewall on the passenger's side, again to drain fuel the short plastic tube projecting from the bottom of the gascolator is pushed up. All three fuel drains should be opened daily prior to the first flight and after every refuelling to check for fuel type/grade, water and sediment.

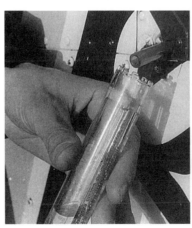

The fuel is drained from the main tank by pushing in the plastic tube.

Drain the auxilary fuel tank by pushing up the inner tube inside the cowling door.

The two fuel tanks are interconnected and supply the engine by a common fuel line, the fuel passes from the tanks to a fuel shut off valve, located behind the passenger's left shoulder, then through the gascolator located on the lower left side of the firewall, forward of the engine, into the carburettor and hence to the engine.

Drain the gasolator by pressing the plastic tube up.

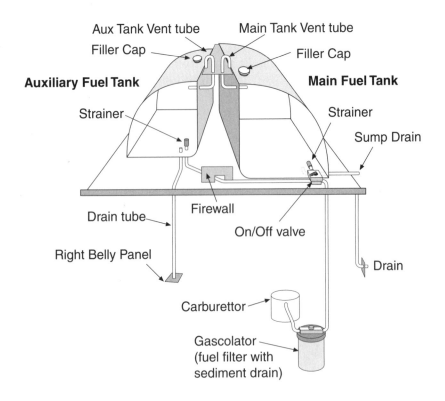

Aux Tank Vent tube   Main Tank Vent tube

Filler Cap

Filler Cap

Auxiliary Fuel Tank

Main Fuel Tank

Strainer

Strainer

Sump Drain

Drain tube

Firewall

On/Off valve

Right Belly Panel

Drain

Carburettor

Gascolator
(fuel filter with
sediment drain)

The Carburettor

The carburettor mixes air with the fuel and supplies the chemically correct fuel/air mixture to the cylinders. The carburettor is located under the engine and takes induction air from a vent aft of the pilot's door. Heated air comes from a scoop placed around the exhaust, the carburettor heat control knob selects the mix of hot and cold air. Unlike most airplanes both hot and cold air are filtered and then fed to the carburettor, the use of the carburettor heat control and carburettor icing are discussed fully, later in this book.

From the carburettor the fuel/air mixture is carried to the induction manifold which feeds the mixture to the intake port of each cylinder. The red mixture control is mounted vertically either forward and to the right of the cyclic, or aft and to the left of the cyclic. In the fully down position the mixture is rich, this is the only position used for flight. Note, unlike airplanes, the R22 pilot does not normally lean the mixture in flight when at altitude. If the mixture control is pulled fully up to the idle cut off position the engine will stop.

The R22 Beta II and Mariner II can be fitted with a vernier mixture control mounted next to the outside air temperature guage. This permits leaning of the fuel/air mixture when operating at high altitudes.

The Engine Governor

The governor maintains engine RPM, and hence rotor RPM, constant through all phases of powered flight. The governor switch is located on the end of the pilot's collective lever and it must be in the on position. The governor senses minute changes in engine RPM and supplies a signal to open or close the throttle to bring the engine RPM back to 104%.

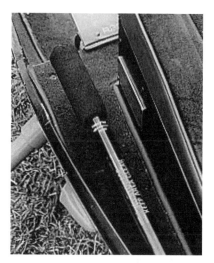

The Twist Grip Throttle

The throttle is located on the end of the collective and controls the engine and rotor RPM. It operates in the opposite sense to a motor bike throttle, rotating one's left thumb down reduces the RPM and rotating ones hand away increases the RPM. The twist grip throttle is

The co pilot's twist grip throttle on the end of the collective.

connected to the butterfly valve in the carburettor via a system of bell cranks and push-pull tubes, there are no cables or gears in the linkage. In normal flight the governor maintains the engine and rotor RPM at 104%. If the governor fails the pilot can control the engine and rotor RPM by use of the throttle. To enable the pilot to practice touch down autorotations, an over travel spring cartridge is located in the vertical linkage. This allows the pilot to roll off the throttle past the idle stop, into the throttle spring detent, which reduces the engine RPM to idle, below the governor operating range. The collective now only controls rotor RPM.

The Electrical System

All R22s use a 14 volt, negative earth, direct current (DC) electrical system, the electrical power is supplied by a 60 ampere alternator, mounted to the rear of the engine on the passenger side, belt driven by the engine. A 12 volt, 25 ampere-hour battery is located either in the nose of the helicopter under the instrument console on standard, HP and Mariner models or just forward and outboard of the engine on the passenger side for Alpha and Beta models.

The alternator is the primary source of power to the electrical system in normal operations, with the engine running, the alternator produces alternating current (AC) which is converted into direct current (DC) by diodes incorporated in the alternator housing which act as rectifiers. By their design alternators require a small voltage (about 3 volts) to produce the electrical magnetic field required inside the alternator. The significance of this is that if the battery is completely discharged (flat) the alternator will not be able to supply any electrical power to

The alternator with the starter motor behind.

the electrical system even after the engine has been started by some other means (external power). Output from the alternator is controlled by a voltage regulator, which is mounted on the right side of the firewall forward of the engine. An over voltage relay is also fitted to protect the electrical system from any over voltage conditions or surges, in the event of a high voltage the relay opens and the alternator becomes isolated, and appears to have failed. The over voltage relay can be reset should this occur by turning off the alternator switch for one second and then turning it back on. Normally the alternator will come back on line and re-supply power to the electrical system. The primary purpose of the battery is to supply power for engine starting, the initial excitation of the alternator and as a back up in the event of alternator failure. In normal operations with the engine running, the alternator provides the power to the electrical system and charges the battery. In the event of an alternator failure, the battery is providing all the power to the electrical system. The ammeter is located on the instrument panel and indicates the current in amperes, to or from the battery. Should the alternator fail, the ammeter will show a discharge, the flow of electricity is from the battery to the electrical system, and the low voltage warning light will illuminate. In this event a landing should be made as soon as possible.

CAUTION

If flight is continued with an inoperative alternator, the battery will eventually lose all its charge and be unable to supply current to the tachometers, producing a very dangerous flight condition.

The pilot controls the electrical system via the red master battery switch, located on the right side of the instrument console. This engages the battery contactor and supplies power to the electrical system.

Due to the importance of the rotor and engine tachometers, these are driven directly from either the battery or alternator, i.e. with both alternator and master battery switches off the two tachometers still operate. The rotor tachometer signal is supplied by a sensor on the input shaft to the main rotor gearbox and the engine tachometer takes a signal from one of the magnetos.

The various electrically operated systems are protected by individual circuit breakers located on a ledge just forward of the passenger seat. The breakers are marked to indicate their function and

The circuit breaker panel located forward of the co pilot's seat.

amperage, and are of the push to reset type. If a circuit breaker pops, wait for a minute to allow it to cool, and reset it. If it pops again, soon after resetting, it should not be reset a second time.

The Warning Lights

Warning lights are located in three places on the instrument panel, along the top of the panel are warning lights for the clutch, main rotor chip, main rotor temperature, tail rotor chip, low fuel and low rotor RPM. Above the engine instruments are warning lights for alternator failure, oil pressure, and governor off. Above the radio and to the right of the panel is the rotor brake warning light.

The clutch warning light indicates the V belts are tensioning or untensioning, if the light flickers or stays on for more than five seconds in flight, it could indicate imminent belt, lower or upper bearing failure.

The low rotor RPM caution light and warning horn activate when the rotor RPM drops to 97% or below.

The oil pressure and low fuel warning lights are independent of the relevant gauges and use separate sensors.

The main and tail rotor chip detector lights are magnetic devices on the drain plugs of both the main and tail rotor gearboxes, any metallic particles in either gearbox are drawn to the magnetic detectors closing an electrical circuit and causing the warning light to come on. This indicates to the pilot the possible impending failure of the gearbox.

The main rotor gearbox temperature warning sensor is located on the main rotor gearbox near the input pinion bearing.

The warning lights are located along the top of the instrument panel, above the the engine instruments and below the magneto key switch.

The alternator warning light indicates low voltage and probable failure of the alternator.

Later helicopters are fitted with a starter and rotor brake warning lights.

The Lighting System

The R22 has a red strobe anti-collision light installed on the tailboom as standard, optional navigation lights are available below both doors, and on the end of the tail. Twin landing lights are installed in the nose, they are set at different vertical angles to improve the pilot's night vision. Having two gives an element of redundancy allowing a safe landing at night to be made even if one light has failed. The instruments and switches are illuminated by post and internal lights, the intensity being controlled by a rotary dimmer switch on the left hand side of the instrument console. These lights only function when the external navigation lights are on. A map light is mounted above and to the left of the pilot's head, should the instrument lights fail the map light can be used to illuminate the instruments.

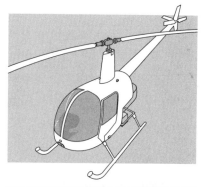

The twin landing lights.

The Pitot Static System

The pitot static system comprises of the pitot tube, the static source and the three pitot static instruments. The altimeter and the vertical speed indicator (VSI) receive static pressure only whereas the air speed indicator receives both pitot and static pressures. The pitot pressure comes from the pitot tube mounted on the front edge of the mast fairing above the cabin, static pressure comes from the static source which is located inside the aft cowl door inboard of the cowl door hinge.

The pitot tube on the forward edge of the mast.

The pitot tube and static source should be checked before flight to ensure they are clear and unobstructed. It is important not to blow into either the pitot tube or static source, as doing so can result in damage to the instruments. Should the readings on the air speed indicator, altimeter and vertical speed indicator become erratic, it could be

The static source inside the aft cowl door inboard of the hinge.

due to water in the lines connecting the pitot tube and static source to the instruments. An engineer can drain the lines by removing plastic drain plugs, accessible through inspection panels on the underside of the cabin.

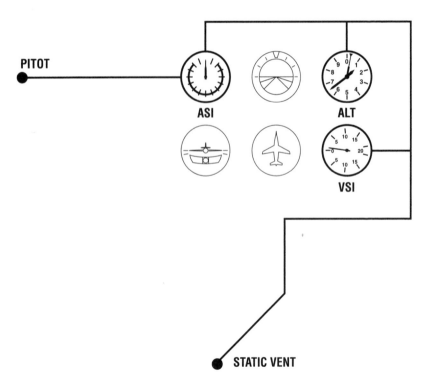

The Heating And Ventilation System

Cabin heating is supplied via a muffler shroud around the engine exhaust system. Air is forced through the shroud by a fan, warmed by the exhaust pipes, and enters the cockpit via a shutoff valve located on the fire wall. It is directed to an outlet in the pilot's footwell, just below the bubble, on earlier models the outlet is from the forward edge of the pilot's seat. The volume of warm air entering the cockpit is controlled by the cabin heat control, mounted on the ledge just forward and below the pilots seat next to the datcon. The cabin heat control is pulled up to select heat, to increase the volume of warm air the fan can be turned on using the fan switch next to the cabin heat control. To turn off the heat the cabin heat control is pushed all the way in and the fan turned off.

The cabin heat controls on the ledge forward of the pilot's seat.

The cabin heat system is very effective once the engine is warm, although it's use is governed by a number of safety factors, as follows;

The heating system effectively opens a path, through the firewall, between the engine bay and the cockpit, and for this reason, the cabin heat is selected to off before engine start, or if a fire is suspected in the engine bay.

With a system of this type there is always a chance of carbon monoxide being introduced into the cockpit. Carbon monoxide is a gas produced as a byproduct of combustion, it is colourless, odourless and tasteless, but a potentially fatal gas. A generally accepted practice is to shut off the heating system if engine fumes (which may contain carbon monoxide) are thought to be entering the cockpit. The danger arises if a crack or split is present in the exhaust system inside the heating shroud, thereby allowing carbon monoxide to enter the heating system.

A carbon monoxide detector.

The use of a carbon monoxide detector is recommended. Most take the form of a stick-on detector with a central spot which turns dark in the presence of carbon monoxide. It is important to make sure that the detector's shelf life is current, this shelf life is indicated on the product packaging.

The ventilation system consists of a fresh air vent situated in the nose, which is opened by pulling the fresh air vent knob situated below the manifold pressure gauge. Additionally, a small vent is located on each door. To provide maximum ventilation these should be wide open in the hover and open about 1 inch in cruise. Alternatively, on a very hot day, either one or both doors may be removed.

When the heating system is in use, the temperature can be set by using a combination of the cabin heat and the fresh air vent in the nose. This reduces the possible danger of carbon monoxide poisoning, and will also prevent the cockpit from becoming stuffy, which could induce drowsiness in the pilot.

Seats And Harnesses

There are two seats in the R22, which are not adjustable, and a cushion is supplied for pilots of short stature, this can be placed behind the pilot in order to reach the pedals. When using the cushion ensure that it does not interfere with the free movement of the collective, which should be able to be fully raised and lowered without restriction. Each seat is equipped with an inertia reel type seat belt, this combines a lap strap with a movable shoulder harness, allowing the pilot unrestricted upper body movement, to operate controls and switches. In the event of an accident the inertia reel will lock, holding the shoulder harness firm, in much the same way as a car seat belt. Note, both seat belts must be fastened for flight, whether with a passenger onboard or solo.

The seats pivot forward about their leading edge to give access to the baggage compartments. Each compartment can hold up to 50lbs of baggage, the maximum seat loading, including baggage, is 240lbs. When loading the baggage compartments it must be remembered that the seat structure is designed to collapse in the event of a heavy landing and hence reduce the impact G load imposed on the pilot. If the baggage compartment is full of non-crushable items, this safety feature no longer applies and the full impact is passed to the pilot via the contents of the baggage compartment. When flying solo, for lateral centre of gravity reasons and for safety reasons, as above, the left baggage compartment is filled first.

Doors And Windows

The R22 has a door each side of the cabin for easy access. To close the door it is gently pulled shut, and then the door handle is pulled back and latched down. To open the door the reverse sequence applies, the door handle is latched up and pushed forward, the door can then be gently pushed open.

Each door has a key lock for security. Certain applications for the R22, such as aerial photography, often require flight with one or both doors removed, this is accomplished by extracting the split pins from the top and bottom door hinges and gently raising the door away from the hinge. Replacing the door is the opposite of removal, the split pins must be installed prior to flight.

The cabin door with the latch in the locked position.

Visibility is excellent from the R22 due to the unobstructed front bubble and large glass areas on the doors. To aid the ability to see aircraft above the helicopter, a skylight is fitted above the passenger's seat. For window cleaning, a soft cloth and warm soapy water is recommended, the use of petrol, alcohol, thinners and window cleaner sprays is not recommended.

Optional Engine Primer System

The optional engine primer system has a primer pump located forward of the pilot's seat near the hour meter. The primer is used to improve engine starting in cold weather, the engine primer is used as follows:

■ Unlock the pump by rotating the handle clockwise until the locking pin disengages and the handle pops out.

■ Pump the handle as required, normally 2 or 3 strokes, for priming.

■ Lock the handle after priming by aligning the locking pin and slot, push down on the handle and rotate approximately 180°.

Optional Rotor Brake

The optional rotor brake is attached to the aft end of the main rotor gearbox and is actuated via a cable connected to a pull handle, located above and behind the pilots left shoulder. Operation of the rotor brake is as follows:

■ After pulling the idle cut-off mixture and stopping the engine, wait 30 seconds.

■ Pull the rotor brake handle forward and down using moderate force, about 10lbs.

■ After the rotor stops, either release the hand pressure and allow the spring pressure to retract the handle or, for use as a static rotor brake, maintain the downward hand pressure and push the bead chain into the slot with your right hand.

■ Ensure the rotor brake is disengaged prior to starting the engine.

Note: An electrical switch activates a rotor brake warning light and also disconnects the starter, preventing an engine start with the rotor brake on.

CAUTION

Applying the rotor brake too soon or using excessive force, i.e. stopping the rotor in under 20 seconds, may permanently damage the brake shoes.

The R22 Mariner

The R22 Mariner and Mariner II are the float equipped versions of the Robinson, enabling landings to be made on water. With this model, Robinson have not just taken an R22 and added floats but have carried out additional modifications. The airframe is modified to provide extra corrosion protection, the air induction system is sealed, the angle of the horizontal stabiliser is altered to +1·8°, and an additional stabiliser at the base of the vertical stabiliser is added for improved controllability and to protect the tail rotor. The battery is located in the instrument console to keep it away from any water spray. The floats are removable in which case the Mariner reverts to an R22 Beta or Beta II.

Section 2
Limitations

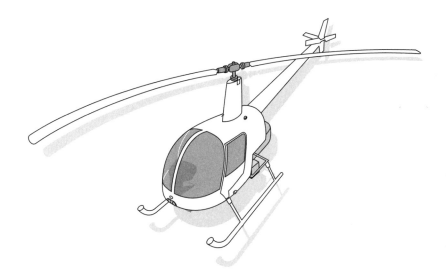

Helicopter Dimensions

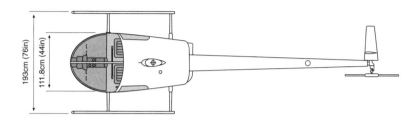

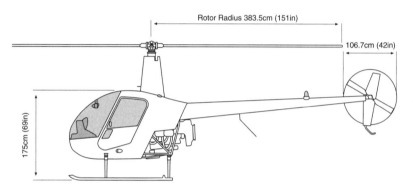

Rotor Radius 383.5cm (151in)

106.7cm (42in)

175cm (69in)

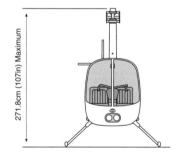

271.8cm (107in) Maximum

The Robinson R22 helicopter is approved under FAA type certificate number H10WE as model R22. Certification is based on a low rotor RPM warning system and an outside air temperature gauge being installed and operative.

The 'V' Airspeed Code

VNO – Maximum structural cruising speed. Do not exceed this speed except in smooth air conditions. This is not a factory limitation but is imposed by the authority to prevent inadvertently exceeding VNE in turbulent air.

VNE – Never exceed speed. Do not exceed this airspeed under any circumstances.

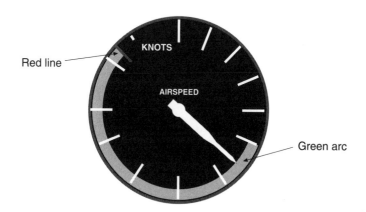

Airspeed Limitations – All R22's with skid gear

(all quoted speeds are knots INDICATED airspeed-KIAS)

VNE up to 3000 feet density altitude 102 KIAS

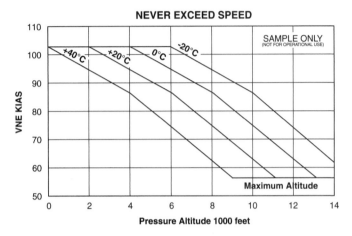

VNO At sea level 92 KIAS

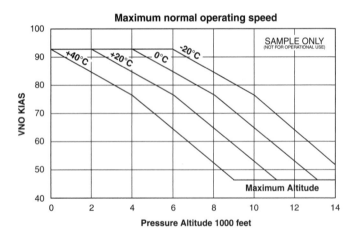

Airspeed Indicator Markings

RED LINE (Never Exceed)	102 KIAS
GREEN ARC (Normal operating range)	50-102 KIAS

Maximum Demonstrated Out Of Wind Component

In The Hover 17 Knots from any direction up to 10,600 feet density altitude

Airspeed Limitations – R22 Mariner with floats

(all quoted speeds are knots INDICATED airspeeds-KIAS)

VNE

Power On up to 3000 feet density altitude	95 KIAS
Power Off up to 7500 feet density altitude	80 KIAS
VNO At sea level	92 KIAS

Airspeed Indicator Markings

RED LINE (Never Exceed)	102 KIAS
GREEN ARC (Normal operating range)	50-102 KIAS

*Note: The colour coding on the airspeed indicator is for a skid equipped Robinson, when using floats the airspeed limitation placard above the pilot's head must be used.

Maximum Demonstrated Out Of Wind Component

In The Hover 17 Knots from any direction upto 10,600 feet density altitude

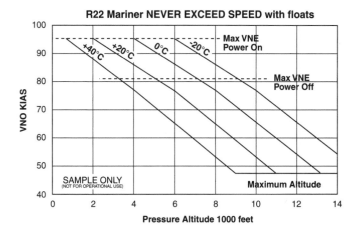

R22 Mariner NEVER EXCEED SPEED with floats

**R22 Mariner II NEVER EXCEED SPEED – KIAS
with floats**

PRESS	OAT -°C						
ALT-FT	-20	-10	0	10	20	30	40
SL							
2000		**95**	SAMPLE ONLY (NOT FOR OPERATIONAL USE)		94	91	88
4000			94	90	86	83	79
6000		90	86	82	78	74	69
8000	86	82	77	72	67	62	57
10000	77	72	66	61	56	51	
12000	66	60	55				
14000	54			NO FLIGHT			

For Autorotation, use 80 KIAS above heavy line

Airframe Limitations

WEIGHTS	lbs	kgs
Maximum Gross Weight – R22 Standard & HP	1300	590
Maximum Gross Weight – R22 Alpha, Beta II & Mariner II	1370	622
Minimum Gross Weight	920	417
Maximum per seat including baggage compartment	240	109
Maximum in each baggage compartment	50	23
Minimum Solo Pilot Weight (no auxiliary fuel)	130	59
(auxiliary fuel)	135	61

Pilots below the minimum pilot weights must carry ballast for the Alpha, Beta and Mariner models. For the Standard and HP models do a weight and balance calculation and if necessary carry ballast.

CENTRE OF GRAVITY (CG) LIMITS

The datum line for the R22 is located 100 inches (254cm) forward of the main rotor shaft centreline.

	Aft of datum	
	inches	cms
Forward CG limit	95.5	242.6
Aft CG limit (Standard & HP)	101.5	257.8
Aft CG limit (Alpha & Beta)	102.0	259.1
Aft CG limit (Mariner with floats)	101.0	256.5
(Mariner without floats)	101.5	257.8

Left CG limit 2.2 inches, (5.6cm), left of helicopter centre line

Right CG limit 2.6 inches, (6.6cm), right of helicopter centre line

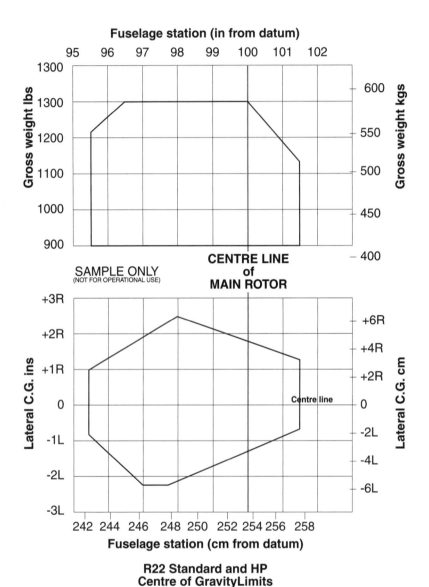

R22 Standard and HP
Centre of GravityLimits

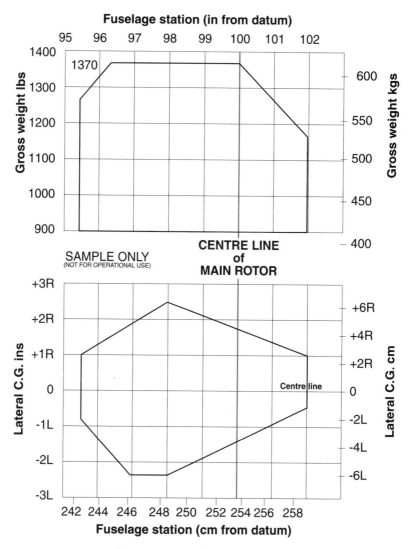

R22 Alpha, Beta and Beta II
Centre of GravityLimits

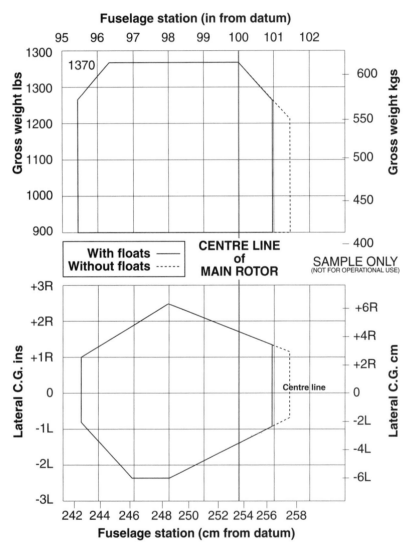

**R22 Mariner and Mariner II
Centre of GravityLimits**

Flight And Manoeuvres Limitations

Aerobatic flight is prohibited

Use maximum power-on RPM, (104%), during take-off, climb, or level flight below 500 feet above ground level or above 5,000 feet density altitude.

Flight in icing conditions is prohibited.

Maximum operating density altitude is 14,000 feet.

Solo flight from right seat only.

Both seat belts must be fastened for flight.

Minimum crew is one pilot, this includes ground running: never leave the helicopter with the engine running.

Doors-off operation is approved with either or both doors removed, under these conditions no loose articles are allowed in the cockpit.

Avoid abrupt pull-ups or push-overs in forward flight, when an abrupt aft cyclic movement is followed by a forward cyclic input a weightless condition can occur. If the helicopter starts to roll during this condition, gently apply aft cyclic to reduce weightlessness before using lateral cyclic to stop the roll.

Operational Limitations

IFR flight prohibited

VFR day is approved

VFR night. The R22 is capable of night operations provided landing, navigation, instrument and anti-collision lights are installed and operable. Orientation during night flight must be maintained by visual reference to ground objects illuminated by lights on the ground or celestial illumination.

The R22 Mariner equipped with floats is not approved for night flight.

Temperature Limitations

Maximum operating ambient temperature   ISA +23°C

Minimum operating ambient temperature   -18°C

Note: these temperature limitations are imposed by the CAA and not the factory.

Wind Limits For Start Up And Shutdown

The rotor must not be started or stopped in steady winds greater than 26 knots or winds gusting greater than 30 knots. These limits again are imposed by the CAA and not the factory

Rotor Speed Limits

	Tachometer reading	Actual RPM
Power On		
Maximum	104%	530 RPM
Minimum	97%	495 RPM
Beta II and Mariner II Minimum	101%	515 RPM
Power Off		
Maximum	110%	561 RPM
Minimum	90%	459 RPM
Rotor Tachometer Markings		
Upper Red Line	110%	
Upper Yellow Arc	104 – 110%	
Green Arc	97 – 104%	
Beta II and Mariner II	101% – 104%	
Middle Yellow Arc	90 – 97%	
Beta II and Mariner II	90% – 101%	
Lower Red Line	90%	
Lower Yellow Arc	60 – 70%	

Engine Limitations

		Instrument Marking
	Tachometer	
Maximum RPM	104%	Red Line
Normal Operating Range	97 – 104%	Green Arc
Beta II and Mariner II	101 – 104%	
	Cylinder Head Temperature	
Maximum	500°F	Red Line
Normal Operating Range	200 – 500°F	Green Arc
	Oil Temperature	
Maximum	245°F	Red Line
Normal Operating Range	75 to 245°F	Green Arc
	Oil Pressure	
Maximum, start & warm-up	100 psi	Red Line
Normal Operating Range	60 to 90 psi	Green Arc
Minimum, idle	25 psi	Red Line

Manifold Pressure

R22 Standard	**0-320-A2B or A2C Engine**
Red Radial	25.9 inches of mercury
Yellow Arc	23.2 to 25.9 inches of mercury

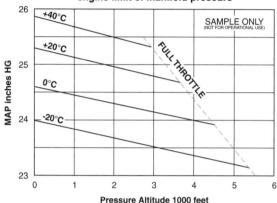

Standard R22 0-320-A2B or A2C engine limit of manifold pressure

R22 HP & Alpha	**0-320-B2C Engine**
Red Radial	24.1 inches of mercury
Yellow Arc	21.0 to 24.1 inches of mercury

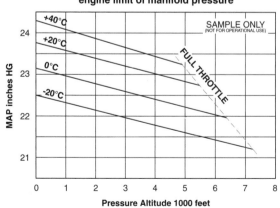

R22 Alpha and HP, 0-320-B2C engine limit of manifold pressure

R22 Beta & Mariner   0-320-B2C Engine

Red Radial   25.2 inches of mercury

Yellow Arc   21.0 to 25.2 inches of mercury

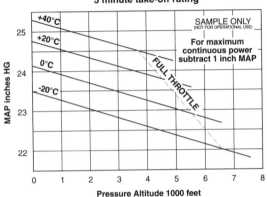

R22 Beta II and Mariner II 0-360-J2A Engine

Red Radial   24.1 inches of mercury

Yellow Arc   19.6 to 24.1 inches of mercury

R22 Beta II and Mariner II MANIFOLD PRESSUR – IN HG

Maximum Continuous Power

PRESS	OAT -°C						
ALT-FT	-20	-10	0	10	20	30	40
SL	21.5	21.8	22.1	22.3	22.6	22.9	23.2
2000	21.1	21.4	21.6	21.9	22.2	22.5	22.8
4000	20.7	21.0	21.2	21.5	21.8	22.0	22.3
6000	20.3	20.6	20.8	21.1	21.3	21.6	21.9
8000	19.9	20.2	20.4	20.7	20.9	**Full Throttle**	

SAMPLE ONLY (NOT FOR OPERATIONAL USE)

For Maximum Take-off Power (5min) add 0.9 IN. HG

Carburettor Air Temperature Gauge

Caution Range   Yellow Arc   -15°C to +5°C

Use full Carburettor Heat On below 18 inches of manifold pressure

Oil Quantity

	US Quarts	Litres
Capacity	6	5.7
Minimum Safe	4	3.8
Note: Dipstick is marked in US Quarts		

Fuel System

Fuel Quantity	US Gal	Imp Gal	Litre
Main Tank Total Capacity	19.8	16.4	74.9
Main Tank Usable Capacity	19.2	16.0	72.7
Optional Auxiliary Tank			
Total Capacity	10.9	9.1	41.2
Usable Capacity	10.5	8.7	39.7
Note: Cockpit fuel gauges are marked in US Gallons			

Float Pressure, Mariner equipped with floats

Maximum Float Pressure   6 psi gauge

Minimum Float Pressure   2 psi gauge

Oil Grades

Average Surface Air Temperature	MIL-L-6082 Straight mineral	Commercial Grade
Above 60°F / 16°C	SAE 50	100
30°F / -1°C – 90°F / 32°C	SAE 40	80
0°F / -18°C – 70°F / 21°C	SAE 30	65
Below 10°F / -12°C	SAE 20	55

Average Surface Air Temperature	MIL-L-22851 Ashless Dispersant	Commercial Grade
Above 60°F / 16°C	SAE 50 or SAE 40	W100 or W80
30°F / -1°C – 90°F / 32°C	SAE 40	W80
0°F / -18°C – 70°F / 21°C	SAE 30 or SAE 40	W65 or W80
Below 10°F / -12°C	SAE 30	W65

SAE 20W-50 approved for all temperatures

Fuel Grades

It is wise to pay attention when your helicopter is being refuelled, especially if at an airfield new to you. More than one pilot has found out to their cost that piston engines designed for AVGAS do not run very well on AVTUR (Jet A-1). To help guard against this eventuality AVGAS fuelling points carry a RED sticker, and AVTUR fuelling points a BLACK sticker.

APPROVED FUEL GRADES

	Engine	Minimum Grade Aviation Fuel
Standard	0-320-A2B 0-320-A2C	80/87
HP	0-320-B2C	100/130
Alpha	0-320-B2C	100/130
Beta & Mariner	0-320-B2C	100/130
Beta II & Mariner II	0-360-B2C	100/130

Section 3
Handling the Robinson R22

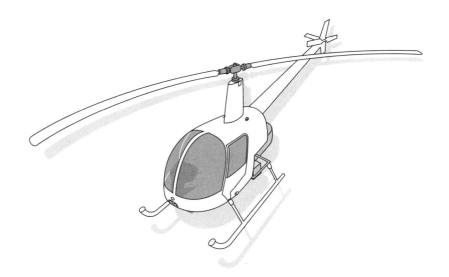

Note: The information in this section is no substitute for flying instruction under the guidance of a flying instructor rated on the R22.

Ground Handling

Due to its light weight and compact dimensions the R22 is very easy for one person to move on its ground handling wheels. The ground handling wheels attach to brackets on the outside, at the aft end, of the two skids.

Ground handling by one person is accomplished by pulling down on the tail rotor gearbox, this lifts the front of the skids clear of the ground, and pushing or pulling the helicopter to the desired area. Note: it is easy to judge obstacle clearance by having the main rotor blades fore and aft, not

Fitting the ground handling wheels.

across the helicopter. The tail fin SHOULD NOT be used for pulling or pushing the helicopter since it imposes undue stresses on the mounting to the tail cone. Should you be fortunate enough to have an assistant, they can help by pushing on the nose when moving the helicopter back, or pushing on the vertical steel tube at the back of the engine bay when moving the helicopter forward. It is not recommended to pull on this tube when pulling the helicopter as the tail of the skid can very easily injure your foot.

Engine Starting

Starting the R22 helicopter is straight forward, the ambient conditions and engine temperature being the principal factors to be considered. Most R22's are not supplied with the optional engine primer, so the engine is primed by fully opening and closing the throttle. Normally 2 to 3 cycles is sufficient but on a cold morning as many as 10 primes may be required. Prior to starting the engine, the throttle is closed against the detent spring. Note: Certain helicopters may require less and others more priming, check with the owner or operator before flying a machine unfamiliar to you. Cranking of the starter should be limited to 10 to 15 seconds, no start usually indicates the engine is over or under primed. Should several attempts at starting be unsuccessful the starter should be allowed a few minutes to cool before attempting a further start. The starter should not be operated after engine start as damage to the starter and flywheel ring gear may result. The starter warning light, if fitted, should go out after engine start: if it remains lit the engine should be shut down immediately.

After engine start the oil pressure should reach 25 psi in 30 seconds, should the oil pressure not reach this within 30 seconds the engine should be shut down immediately. The alternator should be turned on and the ammeter checked, the alternator warning light should go out.

Starting With A Suspected Flooded Engine

An over primed, flooded, engine will be indicated by weak intermittent firing, and puffs of black smoke from the exhaust during the attempted start. If it is suspected that the engine is over primed (flooded) the throttle should be opened 1/4in, the mixture moved to idle cut-off and the engine cranked. If the engine starts the mixture should be moved to the rich position, full in, and the throttle closed slightly to reduce the engine RPM to 50-60%.

Starting In Cold Ambient Conditions (Below 0°C)

Failure to start due to an under primed engine is more likely in cold conditions with a cold engine. An under primed engine will not fire at all, and additional throttle priming is necessary. Starting in cold temperatures will be more difficult due to several factors. The oil will be more viscous, the battery may lose up to half its capacity, the fuel will not vaporise readily and under extremely cold conditions the sparking plugs can ice up. A greater number of throttle primes may be required as discussed above, external power may be needed to supplement the helicopter battery, and pre-heat of the engine may be necessary in very low temperatures.

Power And Pre Take-Off Checks

Once the clutch has fully engaged the engine is warmed up at 70 to 80% RPM until the oil and cylinder head temperatures, and oil pressure are in the green and all warning lights are out. The throttle is opened to raise the RPM to 100%. The magnetos are checked individually, a small drop in RPM is normal and shows that the ignition is functioning properly. No drop at all in RPM when operating on one magneto may well indicate a malfunction in the ignition system, and the possibility that one or both magnetos are staying live. The maximum RPM drop when operating on one magneto is 7% in 2 seconds, with no roughness. An excessive drop in RPM when operating on one magneto, especially when accompanied by rough running, may indicate fouled spark plugs or a faulty magneto.

The carburettor heat is checked, a small drop in RPM should result and the carburettor heat gauge should show an increase in temperature. The subject of carburettor icing is covered more fully later, however an important point to note, especially for airplane pilots, is that the inlet for the hot air is filtered. Carburettor heat can be set partially open and used continually if ambient conditions require it.

The alternator warning light should be checked by turning off the alternator switch, the warning light should come on. If it does not do so, try turning on the landing light.

The low rotor RPM horn and warning light are checked by raising the collective just off the bottom stop and slowly reducing the throttle: the horn/light should come on at 97% RPM.

The sprag clutch (free wheel unit) is checked by closing the throttle smartly with the collective fully down. The engine RPM should immediately drop to idle, and run smoothly. The rotor RPM, due to the inertia of the blades, should fall at a much slower rate, i.e. the needles split.

Prior to take-off the warning lights should all be out, gauges all in the green, carburettor heat above 15°C, sufficient fuel for the flight, radio frequency and volume set, seat belts buckled, doors latched, frictions off, governor on and area clear.

Hovering

The R22 is lifted from the ground to the hover by slowly raising the collective. The cyclic stick maintains ground position and the pedals maintain the desired heading. The helicopter is hovered at a five feet skid height, note this can be reduced to two to three feet once a higher level of competence and proficiency has been obtained. It is not recommended to hover above five feet, as this puts the helicopter in the wrong part of the height-velocity diagram (dead man's curve), since there is insufficient inertia in the main rotor to cushion the landing should the engine fail while hovering.

Hovering close to airplanes should be avoided due to the downwash from the main rotor, this can invert a Piper Cub quite easily. Also downwash picks up dust and small stones which can be a hazard to people and vehicles in the immediate vicinity apart from reducing visibility from the cockpit. Hovering over loose snow can produce white out conditions, leading to the pilot being disoriented and possibly losing control of the helicopter.

Air Taxi

Air taxi is where the helicopter is flown at hover height and walking pace to position from, say, the apron to a suitable area to depart from. Where possible the helicopter is air taxied forwards with the nose pointing in the direction of taxying. The helicopter has the ability to taxi sideways or backwards and these manoeuvres are practised. The preference for taxying forwards is for two reasons: firstly, if the engine fails the helicopter can be run on, if hovering sideways or backwards the helicopter must be stopped prior to ground contact following an engine failure. If this is not done the helicopter is liable to roll over, or pivot backwards about the tail of the skids and cause the tail rotor to make contact with the ground. Secondly, taxying forward gives an unobstructed view of what lies ahead, if air taxying sideways the view is partially obscured and obviously when taxying backwards, the view is totally obscured. Should backwards taxying be required, always do a pedal turn to ensure the area behind the helicopter is clear prior to taxying.

Height-Velocity Diagram

The height-velocity diagram or dead man's curve shows the combination of height and velocity from which an autorotative landing is not possible should the engine fail.

In area A the helicopter is too high and too slow, and in area B too low and too fast.

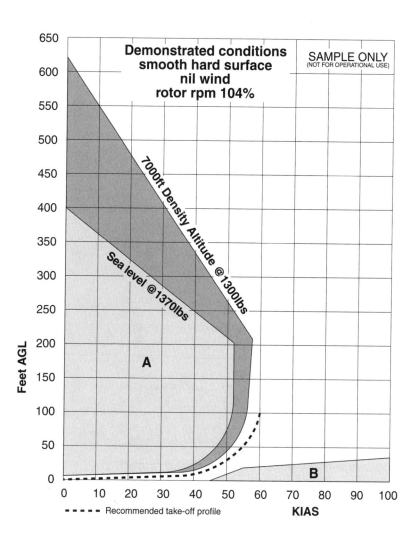

Climb Out

Although the helicopter has the ability to climb out vertically, it is recommended to use a climb out profile that avoids operating in the dangerous portions of the height-velocity diagram.

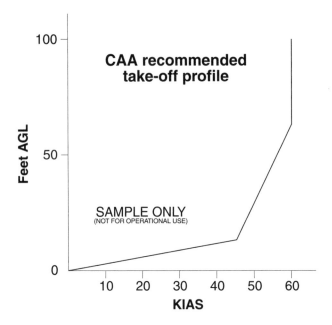

The rotor RPM should be at the top of the green operating range, Robinson recommend that subsequent climb continues at 60 KIAS. Note: the maximum rate of climb, Vy, is a little slower at 53 KIAS.

Cruise

Cruising is normally undertaken with a power setting of 20" to 22" MAP, depending on the gross weight of the helicopter this will give an indicated airspeed of 75 to 85 KIAS. The best range airspeed is 83 KIAS and the maximum normal operating speed is 92 KIAS (Vno) which allows a buffer of 10 knots, for sudden gusts or turbulent conditions (Vne=102 KIAS).

To off-load the high lateral cyclic stick forces to the left in the cruise the trim knob is pulled up.

> ## CAUTION:
>
> On certain R22s the trim knob and mixture are adjacent to one another, to prevent inadvertently pulling the mixture, and stopping the engine, the pilot must reach around the cyclic to pull the trim knob on.

Unlike most airplanes and some helicopters the mixture is not leaned in cruise but left fully rich. However certain R22 Beta II and Mariner II have a vernier mixture control which allows leaning of the mixture when operating at higher altitudes.

Engine Handling

Mechanical engine failures in the R22 are very rare but pilot error can lead to engine stoppage in flight. Most pilot induced engine failures are due to carburettor icing, fuel exhaustion and inadvertent pulling of the mixture control to the idle cut off position.

Having sufficient fuel on board to complete the flight is a point of basic airmanship, accomplished through proper flight planning and thorough pre-flight checks, especially a visual check of the fuel tank contents using a dipstick.

Regular monitoring of the carburettor heat gauge should alleviate the problem of carburettor icing, this is covered in more detail in the next section of this manual.

Regular monitoring of the engine instruments may forewarn of an impending problem. High oil temperature, if not accompanied by a corresponding drop in oil pressure, may indicate a faulty gauge. As with most instances the actions to be taken will depend on the pilot's judgement of the situation at the time. As general guidance a precautionary landing should be made or if local to an airfield, divert to that airfield whilst remaining alert to the possibility of a sudden engine failure. Where high oil temperature is accompanied by low oil pressure, engine failure may very well be imminent, and the pilot should land as soon as possible.

In the event of a low oil pressure reading accompanied by a normal oil temperature reading, again gauge failure may be suspected, a double check would be if the low oil pressure warning light is off or on, since it uses a separate sensor to the oil pressure gauge. Where low oil pressure is accompanied by high oil temperature and the oil pressure warning light is on, engine failure is probably imminent and the pilot should land as soon as possible.

Autorotations

Note: The information in this section is a brief resume of autorotations and is no substitute for flying instruction from an instructor rated on the R22 and reference to the R22 Flight Manual.

A prerequisite for certification of a helicopter is the ability to autorotate (glide) to the ground after an engine failure, and assuming a suitable surface, land without causing further damage to the helicopter. To allow the helicopter to autorotate a freewheel unit, sprag clutch, is placed between the engine and the rotor systems. In the event of an engine failure, the freewheel unit allows both the main and tail rotors to continue rotating. The pilot immediately lowers the collective to reduce the drag on the main blades and adopts an attitude to maintain 65 knots, this results in a steep glide at between 1500 and 2000 feet per minute. The main rotor continues to rotate much as a sycamore leaf does when it falls to the ground.

The helicopter forward speed and rate of descent is reduced at about 40 feet above ground level by applying aft cyclic to flare the helicopter. Then, just prior to ground contact, the cyclic is moved forward to level the skids and the collective is raised to cushion the landing.

CAUTION:

The R22 helicopter has a light, low inertia, rotor system. Most of the energy which is used for completing a successful autorotation is stored in the forward momentum (speed) of the helicopter and not in the rotor. Therefore, a well timed cyclic flare is required with rotor RPM kept in the green until just before ground contact.

Descent And Approach To The Hover

The descent and approach to the hover are performed at 60 KIAS. This will require a manifold pressure below 18 inches, therefore full carburettor heat is applied. Typically a R22 Beta will require approximately 15 inch MAP to achieve a rate of descent of 500 feet per minute at 60 KIAS.

To terminate the approach to the hover, at approximately 200 to 300 feet above ground level the carburettor heat is pushed all the way in, then as the helicopter descends through 100 feet the airspeed is gradually reduced to result in the helicopter coming to a 5 feet hover. As in the take-off, the helicopter should avoid passing through the dangerous portion of the height-velocity diagram. A further consideration is that the rate of descent should be reduced to below 300 feet per minute prior to the airspeed dropping below 30 KIAS, this is to prevent the helicopter experiencing vortex ring.

Landing

The R22 is a very sensitive helicopter to control especially close to the ground. Due to it's narrow skids and light weight the R22 is not very forgiving if ground contact is made whilst moving backwards, sideways or yawing. The R22 should be landed gently but positively either vertically or, if on smooth ground, with slight forward movement. Once ground contact has been made it is not uncommon to assume the flight is over and relax. Then on lowering the collective to the bottom stop, you may find the helicopter yawing through 30° Remember to fly the helicopter from the moment the rotors start turning until they stop turning at the end of the flight.

Due to the R22's very light weight the attitude of the helicopter in the hover is very dependent on the distribution of the weight in the helicopter. This is most noticeable on landing: a pilot flying solo with full fuel will find the helicopter lands on the back of the skids first, whereas two relatively heavy pilots with little fuel will land on the front of the skids first.

Note: Weight and balance is covered in detail in the loading and performance section of this manual.

Parking And Tie Down

When parked outside the R22 should, if possible, be left pointing into the wind. Robinson supply tie-downs to stop the main rotor flapping up and down in a wind. Care should be taken when using the tie-downs, normally the aft blade is tied down to the tail. This should be done by initially pushing up the forward blade, pulling a blade down will damage the flapping restraint mechanism in the rotor hub. Two tie-downs are supplied so if strong winds are anticipated, and the helicopter can not be hangered, both the forward and aft blades can be tied down.

To prevent insects nesting in the pitot tube or static source these can be covered, but remember to remove the covers before flight.

The fore and aft blades tied down.

Section 4
Mixture and Carb Icing Supplement

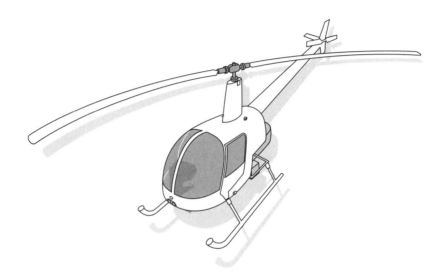

Carburettor Icing

Almost certainly the most common cause of engine rough running, and complete engine failures, is carburettor icing. Despite this, carburettor icing remains a widely misunderstood subject, with many pilots knowledge of the subject being limited to a feeling that the carb heat should be used regularly in flight, without really knowing the symptoms of carb. icing or the conditions most likely to cause its formation.

How Carburettor Icing Forms

IMPACT ICING occurs when ice forms over the external air inlet (air filter) and inside the induction system leading to the carburettor. This type of icing occurs with the temperature below 0°C whilst flying in cloud, or in precipitation (ie rain, sleet or snow). These conditions are also conducive to airframe icing, and the R22 is NOT CLEARED FOR FLIGHT INTO KNOWN ICING CONDITIONS, which clearly these are. So, assuming the aircraft is operated legally within its limitations, this form of icing should not occur, and is not considered further.

Carburettor icing is caused by a temperature drop inside the carburettor, which can happen even in conditions where other forms of icing will not occur. The causes of this temperature drop are twofold:

1. Fuel Icing – the evaporation of fuel inside the carburettor. Liquid fuel changes to fuel vapour and mixes with the induction air causing a large temperature drop. If the temperature inside the carburettor falls below 0°C, water vapour in the atmosphere condenses into ice, usually on the walls of the carburettor passage adjacent to the fuel jet, and on the throttle valve. Generally fuel icing is responsible for around 70% of the temperature drop in the carburettor.

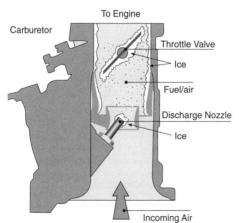

To Engine

Carburetor

Throttle Valve

Ice

Fuel/air

Discharge Nozzle

Ice

Incoming Air

2. Throttle icing – the temperature loss caused by the acceleration of air and consequent pressure drop around the throttle valve. This effect may again take the temperature below 0°c, and water vapour in the inlet air will condense into ice on the throttle valve. This practical effect is a demonstration of Bernoulli's Principle.

As fuel and throttle icing generally occur together, they are considered just as carburettor icing.

Carburettor Icing Conditions

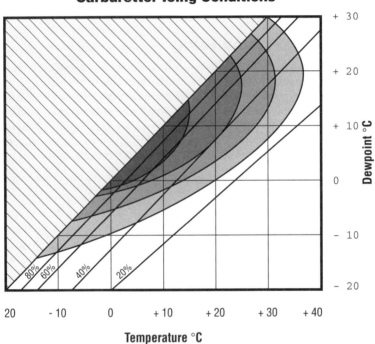

Temperature °C

 100% Relative humidity

Serious icing – any power

Moderate icing – cruise power
Serious icing – descent power

Serious icing – descent power

Light icing – cruise or descent power

Conditions Likely To Lead To Carburettor Icing

Two criteria govern the likelihood of carburettor icing conditions, the AIR TEMPERATURE and the RELATIVE HUMIDITY.

The ambient air temperature is important, BUT NOT BECAUSE THE TEMPERATURE NEEDS TO BE BELOW 0°C, OR EVEN CLOSE TO FREEZING. The temperature drop in the carburettor can be up to 30°C, so carburettor icing can (and does) occur in hot ambient conditions. No wonder carburettor icing is sometimes referred to as refrigeration icing. Carburettor icing is considered a possibility within the temperature range of -10°C to +30°C.

The relative humidity (a measure of the water content of the atmosphere) is the major factor. The greater the water content in the atmosphere (the higher the relative humidity), the greater the risk of carburettor icing. That said the relative humidity (RH) does not to have to be 100% (ie visible water droplets – cloud, rain), for carburettor icing to occur. Carburettor icing is considered a possibility at relative humidity values as low as 30%, it is rare that the RH gets this low in Europe. Herein lies perhaps the real danger of carburettor icing, that it can occur in such a wide range of conditions. Obviously the pilot must be alert to the possibility of carburettor icing at just about all times. Flight in or near cloud, or in other visible moisture (ie rain) might be an obvious cause of carburettor icing, but – VISIBLE MOISTURE DOES NOT NEED TO BE PRESENT FOR CARBURETTOR ICING TO OCCUR.

Symptoms Of Carburettor Icing

The R22 helicopter is fitted with a carburettor heat temperature gauge, this measures the temperature of air in the carburettor. If the temperature remains outside the yellow arc, -15°C to + 5°C, carburettor icing is unlikely to occur, however at power settings below 18 inches MAP, full carburettor heat should be applied. This is because the carburettor heat gauge is not representative of the coldest temperature in the carburettor at low power settings.

Symptoms of carburettor icing are engine roughness and finally engine failure.

Unlike an airplane the R22 engine does not have a propeller bolted onto the crankshaft, so carburettor icing can lead quickly to engine failure, with the intermediate phase of engine roughness being extremely difficult to detect.

Use Of Carburettor Heat

Apart from the normal check of carburettor heat during the pre-flight checks, carburettor heat can be used as is required. The hot and cold inputs both pass through the air cleaner therefore use of carburettor heat when hovering in a dusty environment is no more detrimental to the engine than cold air. Below 18 inches of manifold pressure full carburettor heat must be used, above 18 inches of manifold pressure partial or full carburettor heat can be used continually to keep the carburettor heat temperature gauge reading in the 10 to 15°C temperature range. Since the use of partial or full carburettor heat increases the temperature of the air entering the engine it has a detrimental effect on the power generated by the engine. Hot air is less dense, therefore less mass of air enters the cylinders and less power is generated. The use of carburettor heat does effect fuel consumption, and this may be a factor to consider if the helicopter is being flown towards the limit of its range or endurance in possible carburettor icing conditions.

Care should be taken when flying in extremely cold ambient conditions, below -10°C. In these conditions the use of carburettor heat may actually raise the temperature in the carburettor to that most conducive to carburettor icing. Generally when the temperature in the carburettor is below -8°C moisture forms directly into ice crystals which pass through the carburettor into the engine.

The R22 Beta II and Mariner II are both fitted with carb heat assist. The carb heat assist increases the amount of carb heat applied as the collective is lowered and reduces the amount when the collective is raised.

By transmitting the collective input through a friction clutch the pilot can manually increase or decrease the amount of carb heat for a particular power setting and ambient conditions. The carb heat can be locked off by a latch on the control knob. The control knob should be unlocked when the outside air temperature is between -4 and +27°C and the temperature/dew point spread is less than 11°C.

The Mixture Control

The R22 is supplied with a mixture control, for all modes of flight the mixture is left in the rich position, i.e. in, it is only moved to the lean position, i.e. out, to stop the engine. Therefore unlike an airplane the mixture is not leaned in flight but left fully rich.

However certain R22 Beta II and Mariner II have vernier mixture controls maintained next to the outside air temperature guage. This type of mixture control can be on-wound to lean the fuel/air mixture entering the engine. If you are operating such a model discuss how and when the mixture should be leaned with your flight instructor.

Section 5
Expanded R22 Pre-flight Checklist

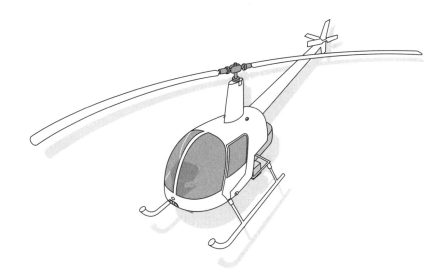

Approaching Helicopter

Remove any covers, tie downs and the wheels if attached.

Look for any oil and fuel spillages from helicopter.

Remove any ice and frost from all surfaces, ensure the numerous control linkage ball joints are not frozen solid.

Check for clear take-off path with particular emphasis on location of other aircraft, the main rotor downwash can invert a light aircraft, loose gravel and other obstructions.

Check maintenance records to ensure helicopter is airworthy.

During the pre flight inspection, check the condition of the helicopter and look for evidence of leakage, heat discolouration, dents, chafing, galling, nicks, corrosion, and most importantly, cracks.

Check for fretting at seams, aluminium fretting produces a black powder, while steel fretting produces a reddish brown or black powder.

'Telatemps' are stick on temperature gauges. They indicate, by turning black, the maximum temperature a component has reached. The engineer places a pencil line after this temperature, i.e. this is the normal operating temperature, should a square beyond the pencil line go black, it indicates the component is running hotter than normal, and an engineer should inspect the component before further flight.

CAUTION:

Do not pull main rotor blades down, as this is likely to damage the flapping restraint mechanism. To lower one blade push the other blade up.

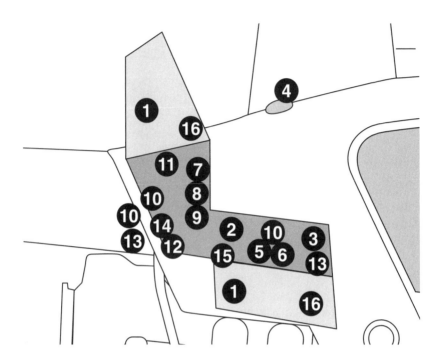

Cowl Door

1. Cowl Doors ....Raise aft and lower forward doors.
2. Auxiliary Fuel Tank ....Check there are no leaks.
3. Auxiliary Fuel Drain ....Raise drain valve and collect fuel from outer pipe, engine side of main firewall, on pilot's side. Check no water or sediment is present.
4. Fuel Cap ....Check fuel contents with the dipstick, ensure the cap is secure.

Note: Auxiliary fuel tank is only fitted to R22 Alpha, Beta and Mariner models.

5. Gearbox Oil ....Check oil level is halfway up sight glass.
6. Oil Leaks...................................Check for any leaks.
7. Rotor Brake ....Mounted at input to main rotor gearbox, check actuation.
8. Flexible Couplings ....Check flexible couplings forward of upper sheave, no cracks and secure. Note: 4 nuts per coupling.

9. Yoke Flanges.............................The yoke flanges are located at the ends of the drive shafts, they are bolted to the flexible couplings, there should be no cracks.

10. Telatemps.................................Located on the main rotor gearbox, the short drive shaft, just forward of the upper sheave, and on the upper sheave bearing. There should be no black squares after the pencil line.

11. Static Source ....Should be unobstructed.

12. Warning Lights...........................Battery switch on, press each button to check circuits and bulbs for: Low Fuel, Tail Rotor Chip, Main Rotor Gearbox Chip and Temperature. Battery switch off. Note: On earlier models the individual sensors need to be short circuited to check continuity of circuits and bulbs.

13. Control Rod Ends ....Free to swivel but no play.

14. Steel Tube Joints.......................Check all welded joints of space frame to ensure no cracks.

15. All Fasteners.............................Visually check screws, rivets, nuts and bolts are secure.

16. Cowl Doors   Both closed and locked.

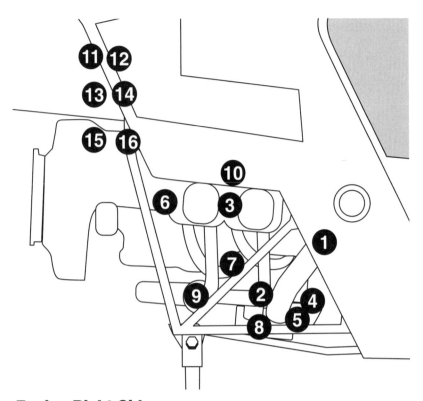

Engine Right Side

1. Inlet Air Duct ....Check security of orange ducting hose, check no blockage of air vent behind pilot's door.

2. Carb Heat Scoop ....Check scoop is secure, with no cracking around the scoop mounting, check orange ducting hose is secure.

3. Cooling Shroud ....These are the grey painted plates ducting cooling air over the cylinders. Make sure no cracks originate from the screw fasteners and screws are present.

4. Electrical Terminals ....Check that the following are secure: Sparking plugs, Cylinder head temperature probe, located on the bottom of the forward cylinder on the pilot's side, Starter motor, Voltage regulator, on the firewall, Starter motor relay and the shower of sparks vibrator.

5. Fuel Leaks...............................Check that there are no indication of fuel leakage from the auxiliary tank, fuel lines and carburettor.

6. Oil Cooler Door.........................Located aft of the aft cylinder on the pilot's side, push open the hinged door and remove any grass or residue on top of the oil cooler.

7. Oil Lines...................................No leaks or chafing of oil lines that run under the cylinders leading to the oil cooler.

8. Air Box Valve............................Only fitted to early models, a spring loaded flap on the bottom of the air cleaner, check that the flap opens.

9. Exhaust System........................Check this is secure with no cracks or visible leaks around the joints.

10. Engine General Condition ....A general check for leaks, missing fasteners, burnt paint and excessive grass blocking the cooling fins.

11. V Belt Condition.........................Rotate top sheave with belts, check no cracks across belts, no excessive wear on inside of belts and they are not too slack.

12. Upper Sheave...........................R22 Service Bulletin 71. Check upper sheave for cracks originating from bolt holes and no grease leakage from bearing on either side.

13. Steel Frame..............................Check no cracks around welded joints and no distortion of tubes, i.e. after a heavy landing.

14. Tail Rotor Forward ....Ensure there are no cracks and the
    Flexible Coupling   4 nuts are secure.

15. Welded Flanges........................Ensure there are no cracks.

16. Tail Rotor Linkage ....Ensure there is no interference, but no excessive play, on the control rod ends.

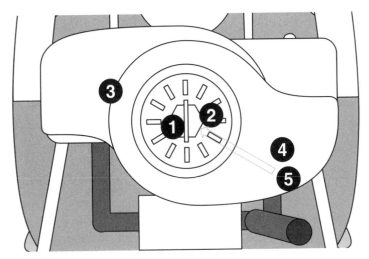

Engine Rear

1. Cooling Fan Nut.........................Split pin must be aligned with paint mark.
2. Cooling Fan ....Check welded fins to ensure no cracking.
3. Fan Shroud...............................Check fibreglass to ensure no structural cracks.
4. Telatemps Lower Bearing..........Both sides must be within 20°C of upper bearing telatemp.
5. Lower Bearing ....Check no grease leakage or seal damage.

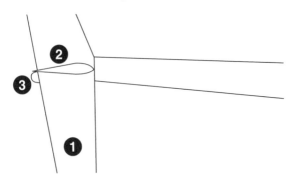

Empennage

1. Tail Surfaces............................Ensure no dents, cracks or ripples.
2. Fasteners.................................Ensure all are tight, with no loose rivets.
3. Position Light...........................Check navigation light on when battery switch on, battery switch off.

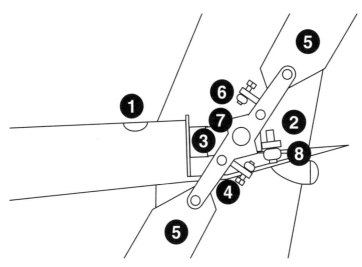

Tail Rotor

1. Aft Flexible Coupling.................Easier to check when on the wheels, pull tail rotor gearbox down, view coupling through window on top of tail cone, rotate tail rotor forward and down. Check 4 nuts are secure and no cracks in the couplings. Note: Do not pull down on the tail surfaces since this applies undue stress to the mountings.

2. Oil Level....................................With tail down, oil should be visible in the site glass.

3. Gearbox Telatemp.....................No increase in temperature.

4. Ground Chip Detector...............Only applicable on early models. Ground chip detector with bulldog clip, battery on check tail rotor chip light on, battery off and remove bulldog clip. Later models have push to test switch inside cowling door.

5. Tail Rotor Blades......................Should be clean, have no cracks and no corrosion on tips

6. Rod Ends.................................Check rod ends of two tail rotor pitch links, should be free, but not loose.

7. Teeter Bearing.........................When blades are teetered as a unit, the ball should not move.

8. Control Bellcrank......................Should rotate freely, but have minimal play in the up/down rocking sense.

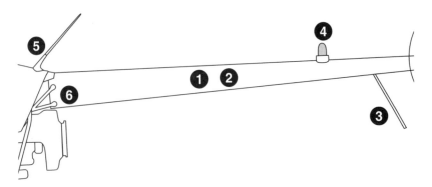

Tail Cone

1. Rivets...Visually check no paint cracks around all rivets, this would indicate a rivet working loose.
2. Skins...No cracks, dents or rippling.
3. Tail Rotor Guard........................Not fitted to early models. Check no cracks along weld and ensure the fasteners are secure.
4. Strobe Light ....Check strobe is secure, not cracked and with battery master on strobe light works, battery master off.
5. Radio Aerial.............................Check clean and no corrosion around mounting at base.
6. Attachment Bolts ....Check fasteners coupling tail cone to fuselage are secure.

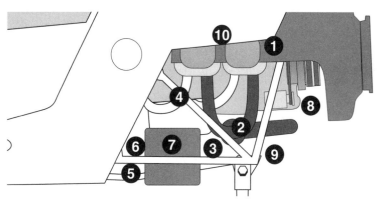

Engine Left Side

1. Cooling Shroud.........................No cracks and all fasteners present.

2. Exhaust System........................Check security, no cracks or visible leakage around joints.

3. Heater Ducting.........................Check that orange ducting from the inlet fan, behind the passenger door, through the exhaust silencer to the firewall is secure and undamaged.

4. Engine Oil................................Yellow dipstick, forward of front cylinder on passenger side, 4-6 US quarts, recommended minimum of 5 US quarts. Do not over tighten.

5. Gascolator (filter).......................Drain and collect, check no water or sediment.

6. Throttle Linkage........................Check operation by twisting (if fitted) throttle and raising collective, and security of fasteners.

7. Battery And Relay.....................Check security of battery, hold down wing nuts and electrical connectors on relay. Note: On R22 HP, Standard and Mariner the battery is under the instrument console in the nose.

8. Alternator.................................Check security of alternator and wiring, ensure belt tension allows about ½ inch of play.

9. Steel Frame..............................No cracks around welded joints and no bent tubes.

10. Engine General Condition ....General check, no leaks, missing fasteners, burnt paint or excessive grass blocking cooling fins.

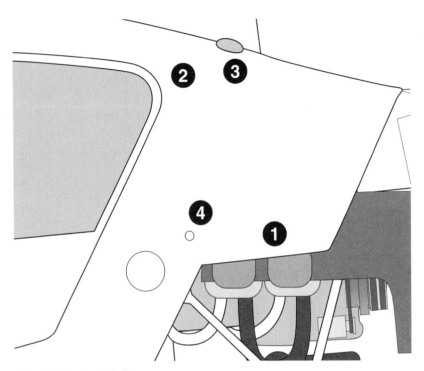

Fuel Tank, Main

1. Leakage......................................Ensure no leakage.
2. Quantity ....Check with dipstick.
3. Filler Cap ....Ensure cap is tight.
4. Drain...Press in the plastic tube sticking out behind the passenger door. Drain and collect the fuel, check there is no water or sediment.

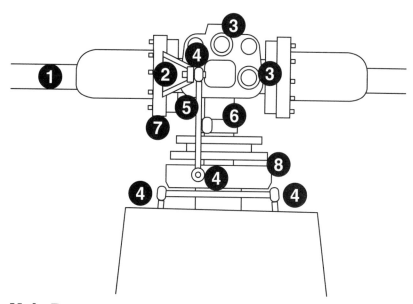

Main Rotor

1. Blades.......................................Ensure these are clean, with no bubbles under the paint, indicating delamination, no cracks along the trailing edge and around stiffeners at root end of blades, and no dents or other damage.

2. Pitch Change Boots..................Ensure no splits or leakage.

3. Main Hinge Bolts ....Ensure nuts are tight and no hair-line cracks in washers on both sides of rotor head, there are 6 washers.

4. All Rod Ends.............................Free but without looseness.

5. Pitch Link Jam Nuts...................Ensure locking nuts on vertical pitch links are secure.

6. Pitch Link Safety Wire ....Ensure vertical pitch links are securely safety wired.

7. All Fasteners............................Ensure all fasteners are tight and secure.

8. Swashplate...............................Ensure that the rubber boot is secure, with tiewraps top and bottom, no leakage or splits. No looseness in swashplate bearings.

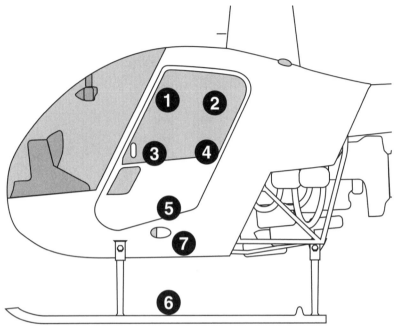

Fuselage Left Side

1. Baggage Compartment ....Check contents. For crash worthiness it should contain the minimum of crushable goods.
2. Collective Control ....Ensure the area around the passenger collective is clear.
3. Seat Belt...................................Must be fastened for flight.
4. Door...Ensure the passenger door is closed and latched.
5. Door Hinge Safety Pin...............Upper and lower hinge must have a split pin installed.
6. Landing Gear............................Check that covers are on end of crosstubes, that crosstubes are not excessively bowed, that the joints top and bottom of the skid uprights are not cracked. Check the skid shoes, on the bottom of the skids, are in place.
7. Position Light............................Check condition and security of position light, with battery master on check operation of light, battery master off.

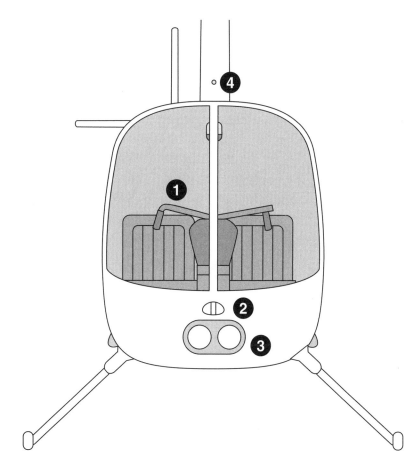

Nose Section

1. Windshield Condition ....Check the windshield is not cracked
   and Cleanliness   and it is clean.

2. Fresh Air Vent............................Ensure vent is clear.

3. Landing Lights ....Check lights are clean and not cracked,
   with battery master switch on check both
   lights function, battery master switch off.
   Note: If the battery is not fully charged
   there may be insufficient voltage to trip
   the landing light relay in which case the
   lights will not function.

4. Pitot Tube ....Check clear of any obstructions.

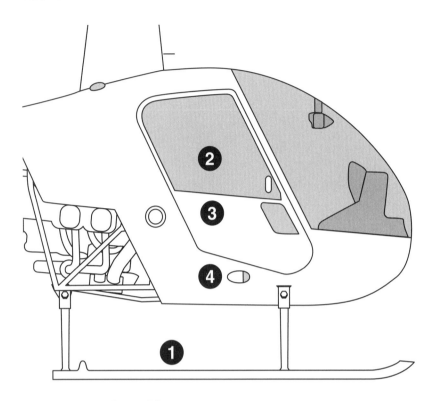

Fuselage Right Side

1. Right Landing Gear ....Check that covers are on end of crosstubes, that crosstubes are not excessively bowed, that the joints top and bottom of the skid uprights are not cracked. Check the skid shoes, on the bottom of the skids, are in place.

2. Right Door Hinge Safety Pins....Upper and lower hinge must have a split pin installed.

3. Baggage Compartment ....Check contents. For crash worthiness it should contain the minimum of crushable goods. Note: When flying solo, fill the left baggage compartment first.

4. Position Light.............................Check condition and security of position light, with battery master on check operation of light, battery master off.

Cabin Interior

1. Fuel Quantity ....Check with Master Battery Switch on.
2. Remove any loose articles ....Removed.
   from cabin
3. Condition Of Seatbelts..............Check operation of latch and no fraying.
4. Instruments, Switches ....Check Condition.
   and Controls

CAUTION:

Short pilots may need to use a cushion to operate all controls to their full limit.

Before Starting Engine

1. Seat Belts ....Fastened.
2. Circuit Breakers ....All in
3. Fuel Shut-off Valve ....On
4. Cyclic/Collective Friction............Off, friction knob forward of cyclic turned fully anti-clockwise and little white wheel on base of collective is hinged forward.
5. Cyclic/Collective/Pedals ....Full free travel of all controls simultaneously.
6. Collective Fully Down ....Friction on, hinge little white wheel aft.
7. Cyclic Neutral ....Friction on, friction knob turned fully clockwise.
8. Pedals.......................................Neutral, both pedals level.
9. Altimeter ....Set to field elevation (QNH) or zero (QFE).
10. All Switches/Avionics.................Off, all rocker switches down and all rotary switches fully anti-clockwise.
11. Clutch ....Disengaged, clutch switch down and clutch warning light out.
12. Mixture......................................Full rich, pushed fully in.
13. Mixture Guard............................Installed, plastic tube placed over mixture control, to prevent inadvertently stopping engine in flight.

Note: Ignore for Beta II and Mariner II fitted with vernier mixture control

14. Carburettor Heat........................Off, pushed fully in.
15. Rotor Brake ....Disengaged, handle fully retracted.

Section 6
Loading and Performance

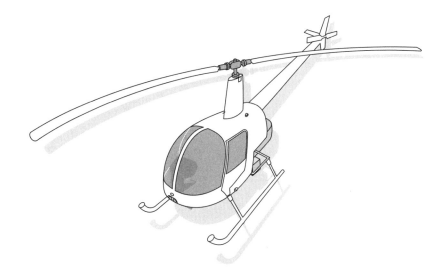

Loading

Helicopter loading can be divided into two areas, the helicopter weight and the centre of gravity (c.g.) position.

The helicopter must be loaded so that its weight is below the certified maximum gross weight (1300lbs/590 kgs for the standard and HP) or (1370lbs/622kgs for the Alpha, Beta or Mariner). The weight limit is set primarily as a function of the lifting capability of the helicopter, which is largely determined by the rotor design and engine power of the helicopter. Operating the helicopter when it is over-weight will adversely affect the helicopter handling and performance, such as:

Exceeding the engine power limits to hover

Increased take-off distance required

Reduced rate of climb

Reduced maximum altitude capability

Reduced range and endurance

Reduction in manoeuvrability and controllability

Insufficient up collective to cushion an engine off landing

Over stressing the rotor system especially under high "g" conditions (i.e. steep turns)

The helicopter must also be loaded to ensure that its centre of gravity (c.g.) is within set limits, normally defined as a forward and aft limit aft of the datum. For this helicopter the datum is located 100 inches forward of the centre line of the main rotor mast. The forward c.g. limit is determined by the amount of aft cyclic available to flare the helicopter and hence stop it. The aft c.g. limit is determined by the amount of forward cyclic available to overcome the tendency for the nose to flap back (pitch up) when subjected to a sudden gust in cruise. An aft c.g. condition is fairly obvious on lifting the helicopter to the hover, the cyclic is way forward and the helicopter hovers with a pronounced tail low attitude. A forward c.g. condition is likely to occur when two heavy pilots arrive at their destination having used up most of their fuel. Initially on take-off they are within c.g. limits, on arrival they find that full aft cyclic will not stop the helicopter.

When loading the helicopter it is standard practise to calculate the weight and c.g. position at the same time, commonly known as the weight and balance calculation, for both the TAKE-OFF and LANDING conditions. Before going further it must be emphasised that the following examples are provided for illustrative purposes only. Each INDIVIDUAL helicopter has an INDIVIDUAL weight schedule that is valid only for that helicopter, and is dependent amongst other things on the equipment fitted to the helicopter. If the helicopter has any major modification, repair or new equipment fitted a new schedule will be produced. Therefore for any loading or performance calculations you must use the documents for the specific helicopter you will be using.

As well as setting out limits the helicopter documents will also give arms for each item of loading. The arm is the distance from the helicopter datum to the item.

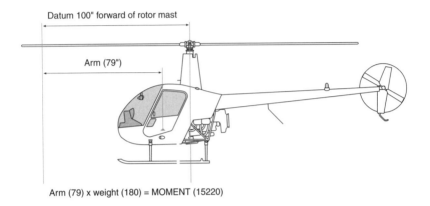

Arm (79) x weight (180) = MOMENT (15220)

The weight multiplied by its arm gives its moment. Thus a set weight will have a greater moment the further away from the datum it is.

The Robinson R22 flight manual will include a centre of gravity moment envelope graph, where the weight can be plotted against the total moment.

The following examples are done using inches and pounds and are based on a R22 Beta with a maximum gross weight of 1370lbs. If you fly a standard or HP then the maximum gross weight is restricted to 1300lbs and a different centre of gravity moment envelope graph must be used.

The operating weight of the helicopter can be split into three categories:-

STANDARD (EMPTY) WEIGHT- the weight of the helicopter, including unusable fuel and full oil. The weight and c.g. position of the helicopter in this condition will be noted in the weight schedule.

VARIABLE LOAD- weight of the crew (i.e. pilot). The certified minimum crew for this helicopter is one pilot (!). The weight schedule will give the arm for the pilot.

DISPOSABLE LOAD- weight of passenger, fuel and baggage. Again the weight schedule will give an arm for each of these loads.

Mathematical Weight and Balance Calculation

With this method of calculation the weights of each item are listed together with their arm. Addition of all weights is the first step, to ensure that the total weight is within the maximum permitted. Assuming this is the case the balance can then be calculated. For each item (except the basic weight where the moment calculation is already done on the weight schedule) the weight is multiplied by the arm, to give the moment. All the moments are added together, to give the total moment, and this figure is divided by the total weight. The resulting figure will be the position of the centre of gravity, which can be checked to ensure it is within the set limits. The weight and total moment can be plotted on a graph in the flight manual. If the plotted position is within the "envelope", the weight and c.g. position are within limits.

To start the pilot will need to calculate a weight for the variable and disposable load. It is obviously important to work in one set of units (either lbs or kgs). This becomes more complicated for the fuel load where volume (litres, imperial gallons or US gallons) will need to be converted into weight. To assist in these conversions, tables are set out in section 8.

Each individual helicopter has an individual weight schedule, valid only for that helicopter. The weight schedule and flight manual will state arms for each item of loading.

ROBINSON R22 Beta - Centre of Gravity Schedule

Longitudinal Weight & Balance
Results must be plotted on C of G graph

	Weight x	Arm =	Moment
Empty Wt of Aircraft	(A)		(B)
Pilot + *Passenger* + Baggage		78.0	
Empty C.G			
Main Fuel (6lbs/USG)		108.6	
Aux Fuel		103.8	
Full C.G.			

Lateral Weight and Balance

	Weight x	Arm =	Moment
Empty Wt of Aircraft			
Pilot + Baggage		+10.7	
Passenger + Baggage		-9.3	
Empty C.G.			
Main Fuel		-11.0	
Aux Fuel		+11.2	
Full C.G.			

Weights and Moments (*Examples*)

Aircraft Regn	Empty Weight (A)	Moment (B)
G-G8FC	857.9lbs	89116.31 inch Lbs
G-INGB	866.8lbs	90252.50 inch lbs
G-ELFI	862.4lbs	89823.75 inch lbs
G-JWFT	862.8lbs	89732.00 inch lbs

EXAMPLE

Helicopter – A

The following figures are used to complete a weight schedule for helicopter A. These figures are put into the table to check the weight and balance.

Empty Weight	862.4 lbs
Moment	89 823.75 inch lbs
Pilot Weight	170 lbs
Passenger Weight	150 lbs
Main Fuel Tank	19.2 USG (6 lbs/USG)
Aux Fuel Tank	10.5 USG (6 lbs/USG)

The moment is calculated by multiplying the weight by the arm. The figure for the arm is found in the R22 flight manual.

Centre of Gravity is calculated by dividing the moment by the weight.

Longitudinal Weight & Balance

	Weight	Arm	Moment
Empty Weight of Aircraft	862.4	0	89 823.75
Pilot + Passenger + Baggage	320.0	78.0	24 960.00
Empty Centre of Gravity	1182.4	97.08	114 783.75

Therefore helicopter A has a centre of gravity with no fuel on board of 97.08 inches (E)

	Weight	Arm	Moment
Main Fuel	115.2	108.6	12 510.72
Aux Fuel	63.0	103.8	6 539.40
Full Centre of Gravity	1360.6	98.36	133 833.87

Therefore helicopter A has a centre of gravity, with full tanks of fuel on board of 98.36 inches (F)

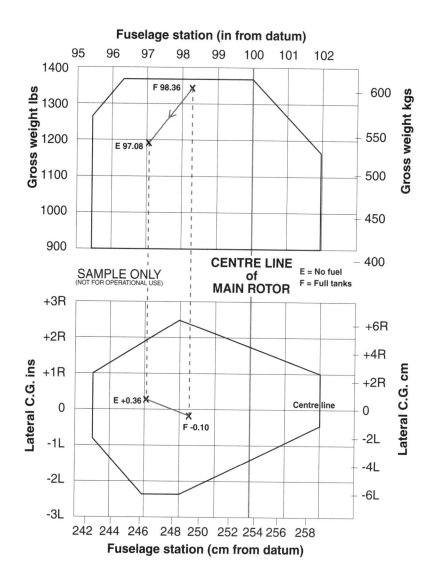

Lateral Weight & Balance

	Weight	Arm	Moment
Empty Weight of Aircraft	862.4	0	0
Pilot + Baggage	170.0	+10.7	+1819.0
Passenger + Baggage	150.0	-9.3	-1395.0
Empty Centre of Gravity	1182.4	+0.36	+424.0

The lateral centre of gravity with empty fuel tanks is +0.36, which is to the right of the centre line.

	Weight	Arm	Moment
Main Fuel	115.2	-11.0	-1267.2
Aux Fuel	63.0	+11.2	+705.6
Full Centre of Gravity	1360.6	-0.10	-137.6

The lateral centre of gravity with full fuel tanks is – 0.10, which is to the left of the centre line.

Using the R22 Alpha & Beta Centre of Gravity Limits graph, mark the lateral centre of gravity. Extend the lines down from the top section to the bottom section. Marking E and F.

When all these lines are plotted on the graph, it can be seen that the c.g. position is within the envelope and therefore within limits.

EXAMPLE 2: Helicopter – A

The following figures are used to complete a weight schedule for helicopter A. These figures are put into the table to check the weight and balance.

Empty Weight	862.4 lbs
Moment	89 823.75 inch lbs
Pilot Weight	240 lbs
Passenger Weight	240 lbs
Main Fuel Tank	19.2 USG (6 lbs/USG)
Aux Fuel Tank	10.5 USG (6 lbs/USG)

The moment is calculated by multiplying the weight by the arm. The figure for the arm is found in the R22 flight manual.

Centre of Gravity is calculated by dividing the moment by the weight.

Longitudinal Weight & Balance

	Weight	Arm	Moment
Empty Weight of Aircraft	862.4	0	89 823.75
Pilot + Passenger + Baggage	480.0	+8.0	37 440.00
Empty Centre of Gravity	1342.4	94.80	127 263.75

Therefore helicopter A has a centre of gravity with no fuel on board of 94.80 inches (E)

	Weight	Arm	Moment
Main Fuel	115.2	108.6	12 570.72
Aux Fuel	63.0	103.8	6539.40
Full Centre of Gravity	1520.6	96.22	146 313.87

Therefore helicopter A has a centre of gravity, with full tanks of fuel on board of 96.22 inches (F)

Using the following chart – R22 Alpha & Beta Centre of Gravity Limits plot E and F

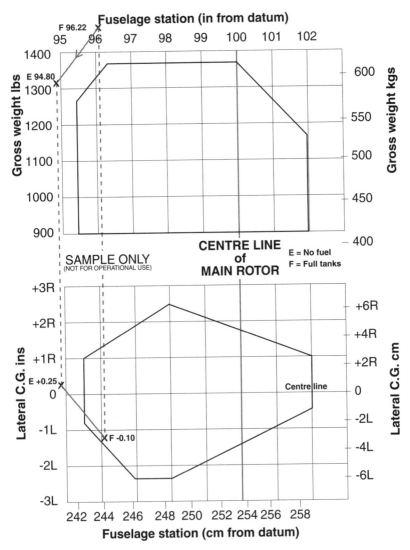

R22 Alpha, Beta and Beta II
Centre of GravityLimits

Lateral Weight & Balance

	Weight	Arm	Moment
Empty Weight of Aircraft	862.4	0	0
Pilot + Baggage	240	+10.7	2568.0
Passenger + Baggage	240	-9.3	-2232.0
Empty Centre of Gravity	1342.4	+ 0.25	+336.0

The lateral centre of gravity with empty fuel tanks is +0.25 which is to the right of the centre line.

	Weight	Arm	Moment
Main Fuel	115.2	-11.0	-1267.2
Aux Fuel	63.0	+11.2	+705.6
Full Centre of Gravity	1360.6	-0.10	-137.6

The lateral centre of gravity with full fuel tanks is -0.10, which is to the left of the centre line.

Using the R22 Alpha & Beta Centre of Gravity Limits graph, mark the lateral centre of gravity. Extend the lines down from the top section to the bottom section marking E and F.

When all these lines are plotted on the graph, it can be seen that the c.g.position is outside the envelope and therefore not within safe operating limits.

A WORD OF WARNING

As well as the safety aspect, operating a helicopter outside its weight and balance envelope has far-reaching legal and financial implications. Almost the first thing an accident investigator will check after an accident is the loading of the helicopter. If the loading is outside limits the pilot is contravening aviation law. In addition both the helicopter's insurance company and the pilot's personal insurance company will be unsympathetic when they know that the conditions of the Certificate of Airworthiness (i.e. the flight manual limitations) were not complied with. As the pilot in command you are responsible.

Performance

The R22 flight manual contains a section of graphs to allow the pilot to calculate the expected performance of the helicopter, in addition to the performance section, there may be a supplement section containing additional performance data from the certifying authority. Two things to remember: firstly the flight manual performance is obtained by using the recommended techniques – to get graphical results use graphical procedures. Secondly the performance section data was obtained under ideal conditions, with a new helicopter and an experienced test pilot. To make allowances for a less than new helicopter, being flown by an average mortal in the real world it is wise to 'factor' any results you get. As with loading calculations the pilot must use the graph and data from the documents for the individual helicopter being used. The graphs and data used in this section are for illustrative purposes only, and not for operational use.

General

Hovering has been demonstrated in 17 knot winds from any direction up to 10,600 feet density altitude. Note that this is not a limitation but a FAA requirement for initial certification, depending upon pilot capabilities controllability is possible in stronger winds.

Use maximum ROTOR RPM (104%) during take-off and flight below 500 feet AGL or above 5,000 feet density altitude.

Hover performance graphs were obtained with carburettor heat OFF.

Adequate engine cooling has been obtained to an outside air temperature of 38°C at sea level or 23°C above standard ISA at altitude.

The graphs and data for the R22 BETA are used as examples in this section. It is essential to refer to the similar graphs and data in the helicopter flight manual for the helicopter you will be flying.

Hovering In Ground Effect Calculation Example

For this example we will take the condition as:

Pressure Altitude 9000ft

Outside air temperature +10°C

Firstly go to the 9000ft Pressure Altitude line and move horizontally across to intercept the +10°C temperature curve. Then move vertically down and read off the maximum gross weight of 1230lbs.

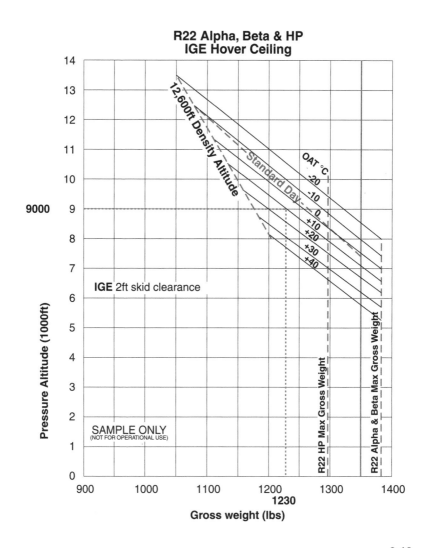

Hover Out Of Ground Effect Calculation Example

For this example we will take the conditions as :

    Pressure Altitude 9000ft

    Outside Temperature +10°C

The helicopter flight manual contains two graphs for hovering out of ground effect for the R22 Beta, one for maximum continuous power and one to take advantage of the five minute take-off rating. We will consider the maximum continuous power graph for this example.

As with the HIGE example we firstly go to the 9000 feet pressure altitude line then move horizontally across to intercept the +10°C temperature curve. Finally move vertically down to read off the maximum gross weight of 1150lbs.

R22 Alpha, Beta & HP
OGE Hover Ceiling
Max Continuous Power

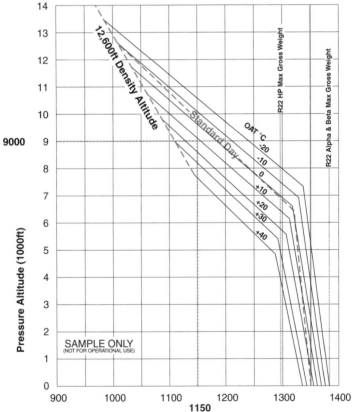

Height-Velocity Diagram

The height-velocity diagram shows the combinations of height above ground and velocity from which a successful autorotation to the ground is not possible. When operating in the upper left hand area the helicopter is too high and too slow whereas in the lower right hand area the helicopter is too low and too fast. For the helicopter to take-off it can be seen it must accelerate to 45 knots then commence a climb while accelerating to 60 knots. Similarly on approach 60 knots is maintained to a height of approximately 100 feet, then the helicopter is decelerated to the hover.

The UK's Civil Aviation Authority (CAA) supply a recommended take-off profile, which for a R22 weighing 1300lbs and using maximum continuous power gives a take-off distance, to a height of 100 feet, of 1200 feet. This distance will vary with pressure altitude, temperature, helicopter weight, wind and in the case of the Beta the 5 minute take-off power rating.

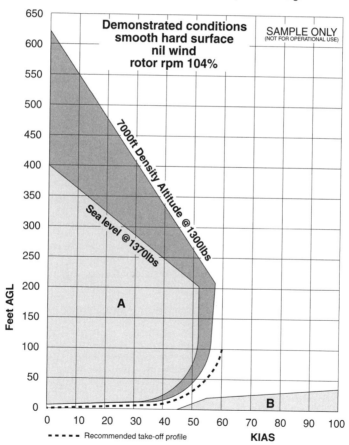

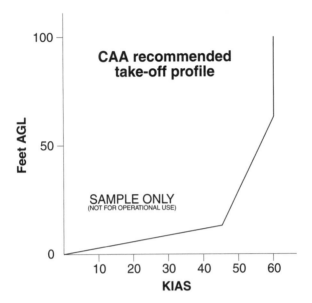

Cruise Performance

The R22 flight manual gives very little information on cruise performance apart from giving the maximum range speed of 83 knots. It is common practice to cruise with a given manifold pressure, typically 20 inches, the resulting airspeed being inversely proportional to the gross weight (20 inches typically yields a true airspeed between 70-85 knots). From experience, cruising at 20 inches of manifold pressure consumes approximately 8 US Gallons per hour. Obviously the fuel burn of different helicopters operating under different conditions will vary, YOU MUST CONSULT THE OPERATOR OR USE YOUR EXPERIENCE OF THE PARTICULAR HELICOPTER FOR ITS FUEL CONSUMPTION.

Autorotational Performance

A CAA supplement includes a graph showing autorotational glide performance. This shows the horizontal distance covered in the glide to sea level following an engine failure at altitude. The following conditions apply:

> Engine – Inoperative
>
> Rotor – 90% rpm
>
> Airspeed – 65 KIAS
>
> No wind

Autorotational Performance Calculation

The following conditions apply:

> Cruise Altitude 6000 feet
>
> Ground Altitude 1000 feet

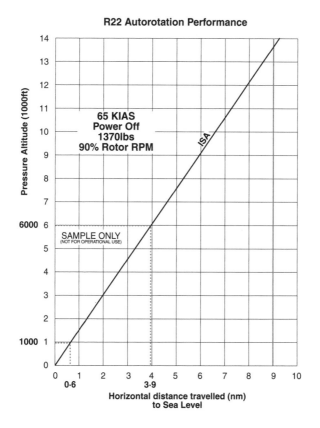

R22 Autorotation Performance

To obtain the glide distance to an altitude other than sea level, the calculation is performed twice. Firstly the glide distance to sea level from cruise is found, then the glide distance from ground level to sea level is found and deducted to give the glide distance to the ground.

From 6000 feet move horizontally to intercept the 'ISA' line then move vertically down to read-off the glide distance to sea level of 3.9 nautical miles. Similarly from 1000 feet to sea level gives 0.6 nautical miles. Hence the glide distance from 6000 feet to the ground elevation of 1000 feet is 3.3 nautical miles.

Helicopter Site Characteristics

Touchdown and Lift-Off Area (TLOF)

The TLOF is the area used by the helicopter to take-off, land, and embark and disembark passengers. It must be large enough to contain a circle of a diameter of at least twice the overal length of the helicopter including the rotors. It shall be free of obstructions, capable of supporting the helicopter and free of loose particles that can be blown around by the rotor downwash.

Take-Off Distance Available (TODA)

The TODA is the total length encompassing the Horizontal Acceleration Area (HAA) and Take-Off Area (TA).

The HAA is an unobstructed area for the helicopter to accelerate to climb speed, it must be 60 metres wide or three times the length of the helicopter including rotors, which ever is greater. It must be suitable for an emergency landing.

The TA is the area beyond the HAA for the helicopter to iniate its climb to 100 feet above the surface. The helicopter shall have sufficient performance to clear any obstructions in the TA by 35 feet, its lateral dimensions shall be at least that of the HAA.

Take-Off Climb Area (TOCA)

The TOCA is the area beyond the TA which contains areas suitable for emergency landings and allows the helicopter to climb to its normal operating altitude.

Inner Approach Area (IAA)

The IAA is the area over which the helicopter can descend below 100 feet during its approach to land. The IAA shall have a minimum width of 60 metres or three times the helicopter length, including the rotors, whichever is the greater and long enough to contain the landing distance for the helicopter. The helicopter shall have sufficient performance to clear all obstacles in the IAA by 35 feet.

Approach Area (AA)

The AA is the area before the IAA in which the helicopter can descend to a minimum height of 100 feet above the surface which contains suitable areas for emergency landings.

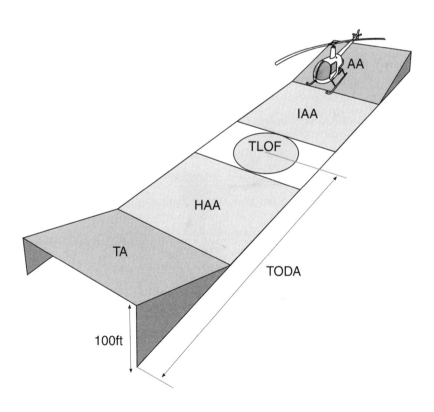

Robinson Safety Notices

At the back of the Robinson flight manual there is Section 10, SAFETY TIPS AND NOTICES, **these safety notices MUST be read by ALL Robinson Pilots,** they contain valuable information gained by the experience of others. Listed below are very brief resumes of these safety notices:

SN-1   Inadvertent use of mixture control in flight
Precautions when trailering helicopter

SN-9   Many R22 accidents involve dynamic roll-over

SN-10 Fatal accidents caused by failure to lower collective

SN-11 Abrupt pull-ups and push-overs can be catastrophic

SN-13 Use of carburettor heat
Do not attach items to the skids
Caution during ground handling

SN-15 Fuel exhaustion can be fatal
Students unprepared for solo

SN-16 Power lines are deadly

SN-17 Never exit helicopter with engine running
Hold controls firmly when boarding passengers
Do not experiment with low-G manoeuvres

SN-18 Loss of visibility can be fatal
Over-confidence still prevails in R22 accidents

SN-19 Low flying over water very hazardous

SN-20 Beware demonstration or initial training flights

SN-22 Always reduce rate of descent before reducing airspeed

SN-23 Walking into tail rotor can be fatal

SN-24 Low rpm rotor stall can be fatal

SN-25 Carburettor ice season is here

SN-26 Night flight plus weather is deadly

SN-27 Surprise throttle chops can be deadly

SN-28 Listen for impending bearing failure
Detecting bearing noise
Flickering clutch light
Do not rely on telatemps

SN-29   Airplane pilots high risk when flying helicopters

SN-30   Loose objects can be fatal

SN-31   Governor can mask carb ice

SN-32   High winds and turbulence

SN-33   V belts turning rotor on startup

SN-34   High risk during photo flights

SN-35   Flying near broadcast towers

SN-36   Overspeeds on lift-off

SN-37   Exceeding approved limitations can be fatal

Section 7
Robinson R22 Awareness Training

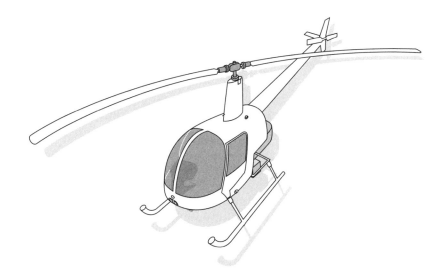

In January 1995 after pressure from the National Transportation Safety Board (NTSB), the FAA in the USA issued an amendment to the limitations of the R22. The background to this amendment was the high number of fatal accidents affecting the R22 in the USA. In February 1995 the FAA then issued SFAR73, covering the ground and flight training required to be undertaken by ALL FAA pilots wishing to fly the R22 helicopter. In March 1995 the FAA relaxed this amendment provided the pilot had attended an awareness training course and had 200 hours of helicopter flight time which included 50 hours in the R22.

The following paragraphs cover the ground school subjects described in SFAR73.

Energy Management
Engine Failure

Energy management when applied to the failure of the engine of a single engine helicopter can be considered under 2 headings:

> Potential energy, this is the energy the helicopter possesses due to its height above the landing site.

> Kinetic energy, this is the energy of the helicopter due to its speed through the air.

On experiencing an engine failure, the pilot lowers the collective allowing the helicopter to use its potential energy to descend down through the air, this flow of air up through the rotor disc causes the rotor to autorotate and allows the helicopter to descend in a controlled manner albeit at a fairly high rate of descent.

As the helicopter approaches the ground the pilot utilises the kinetic energy of forward flight, by flaring, to:

> Reduce the ground speed.

> Reduce the rate of descent.

> Increase the rotor RPM and the rotor's inertia.

This rotor inertia is used, as the helicopter is levelled, to keep the rotors spinning as the pilot raises the collective to generate the rotor thrust to cushion the landing.

Obviously the store of potential and kinetic energy is dependant upon the particular operation the helicopter is performing. The height velocity diagram (dead man's curve) shows the areas of operation where the combination of potential and kinetic energy is insufficient to allow a safe landing of the helicopter if the engine fails.

Robinson recommend an autorotation speed of 65 knots, this gives a compromise between glide angle and rate of descent.

Low Rotor RPM

The energy in the rotor system is proportional to the rotational velocity squared, i.e. at 104% the rotor has 15% more energy than at 97%. Due to the low inertia of the rotor system, the rotor RPM tends to drop very rapidly when the pilot decreases the throttle or abruptly raises the collective. This also occurs when the rotor disc becomes unloaded.

If the pilot attempts to increase the lift of the helicopter by raising the collective when a low rpm condition exists he only makes matters worse:

■ Energy required to accelerate the blades to the top of the green band, also

■ the higher pitch angle on the blades has increased the drag of the blades. It is now possible that the engine will have insufficient power to accelerate the rotors and the RPM will decay further.

Lift can be generated with either a high velocity and low angle of attack, the preferred method – or a low velocity and a high angle of attack. The highest Lift/Drag ratio occurs with a small angle of attack, this is the rotor acting at its most efficient. As the angle of attack increases more and more power is required to generate the same lift and to overcome the increasing rotor drag.

Mast Bumping

Helicopters with teetering rotor heads are susceptible to mast bumping, this occurs when the helicopter is subjected to a zero G manoeuvre, such as an abrupt pushover.

With a teetering rotor head the helicopter fuselage adopts a similar attitude to the rotor disc due to the moments formed between the rotor thrust and the helicopter's weight and drag acting through the c.g.

In the case of a zero G manoeuvre, the rotor disc is generating no rotor thrust, the helicopter is weightless, therefore any inputs from the pilot with the cyclic will affect the rotor disc but not the fuselage. Mast bumping usually occurs when the helicopter rolls under a zero G condition and the pilot attempts to level the helicopter with opposite lateral cyclic. This has no effect on the fuselage but causes the rotor disc to flap sideways more until the rotor hub hits the rotor mast with disastrous results.

The correct action on encountering a low G condition is to apply aft cyclic to load the rotor disc, once the cyclic has control over the fuselage gently apply forward or lateral cyclic as required to resume normal flight.

Note: ■ do not apply full aft cyclic

■ there will be a short delay before the helicopter responds to the cyclic input

■ use of full cyclic could cause the main rotor to impact the tail boom.

Low Rotor RPM (Blade Stall)

Helicopter pilots are familiar with retreating blade stall which is one of the factors limiting the forward speed of the helicopter but little is known of blade stall at low rotor RPM.

The lift and drag equations can be summarised as follows:

Lift is proportional to Velocity squared and the Coefficient of Lift which varies with angle of attack.

Drag is proportional to Velocity squared and the Coefficient of Drag which varies with angle of attack.

A low angle of attack gives proportionally more lift than drag whereas a high angle of attack does the opposite. At high angles of attack, pulling a lot of collective, the engine is using a large proportion of its power to overcome the drag of the blades.

If the pilot finds the helicopter is settling the immediate reaction is to pull more collective. However, if the rotor RPM is low the engine may not have sufficient power to overcome the increased rotor drag and the rotor RPM will decrease further. This results in a further loss of lift leading the pilot to pull more collective and eventually a point is reached where the rotor blades stall.

This stalling is not symmetrical across the disc, the retreating blade is affected the most due to the lower velocity across it resulting from forward flight, and it tends to flap down towards the tail. The advancing blade flaps up to reduce its lift to balance the loss of lift of the retreating side. The helicopter is now descending quite rapidly and the airflow impacting the horizontal tail surface tends to lift the tail resulting in a nose low dive. Combined with the disc flapping back and the pilot applying aft cyclic to attempt to stop the nose dropping this is likely to result in the main rotor hitting the tail boom.

The correct action on encountering a reduction in rotor RPM is to apply throttle, and if the rotor low RPM light and horn are on lower the collective slightly to reduce the pitch, angle of attack and hence the rotor drag. This will enable the increase in engine power to bring the rotor RPM back to the top of the green band. Additionally, if the low RPM condition occurs in forward flight a light application of aft cyclic will load the disc and result in an increase in rotor RPM.

Aeroplane pilots must be trained so that the above recovery procedure is used instinctively when they hear the low RPM horn. This horn sounds like the stall warning on an aeroplane where the corrective action is to dive the aircraft to recover from the stall. In a helicopter this reaction would, by unloading the rotor disc, reduce the rotor RPM further.

Low G Hazards

Low G hazards occur when the rotor disc becomes unloaded or partially unloaded, this may occur in turbulent conditions when the helicopter is suddenly subjected to a down draught, or when the pilot executes a push over.

In the case of a zero or very low G condition the helicopter is liable to roll to the right due to the tail rotor force, which is above the c.g., having no or very little opposing force from the main rotor. The pilot should not attempt to correct this roll with left cyclic, since mast bumping could occur. He should apply aft cyclic to load the rotor disc and recover the lost rotor thrust, then control of the fuselage attitude will return to normal.

Aeroplane pilots are susceptible to creating a dangerous low G situation if, on seeing another aircraft conflicting with their flight path, they apply forward cyclic abruptly to dive the helicopter clear. The recommended procedure is to either turn the helicopter or enter an autorotation if a loss of height is deemed the best avoiding action.

Rotor RPM Decay

The Robinson is designed so that a lowering of the collective under normal operating conditions will cause the rotor RPM to decay slightly, and the opposite occurs when raising the collective.

When making a fairly large power change, such as establishing an approach to a landing site, in addition to lowering the collective a slight increase in throttle will be required to keep the rotor RPM at the top of the green band. On executing the flare at the termination of the approach, the rotor RPM is likely to rise into the red requiring a reduction of throttle. On entering the hover this reduction in rotor RPM must now be compensated for by the addition of throttle. If the pilot has not been concentrating on the rotor RPM during the approach he may well have failed to add throttle to maintain the RPM at the top of green band. Thus in the flare the rotor RPM may be at the top of the green band but on entering the hover additional throttle will be needed.

Rotor RPM decays rapidly in the Robinson due to its low inertia rotor system, the prime causes for this decay are:

■ Applying excessive up collective when the rotor RPM is low and the engine is already generating a lot of power.

■ Inadequate pilot control of throttle when executing large power changes.

■ Subjecting the helicopter to low G manoeuvres.

■ Applying excessive up collective in an autorotation when too high above the ground.

Section 8
Conversions

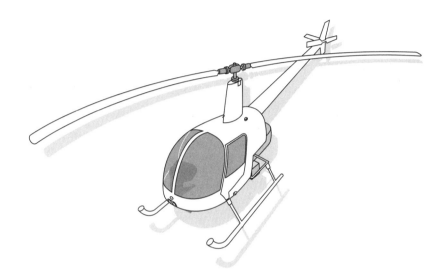

Wind Component Graph
17kts advised limit

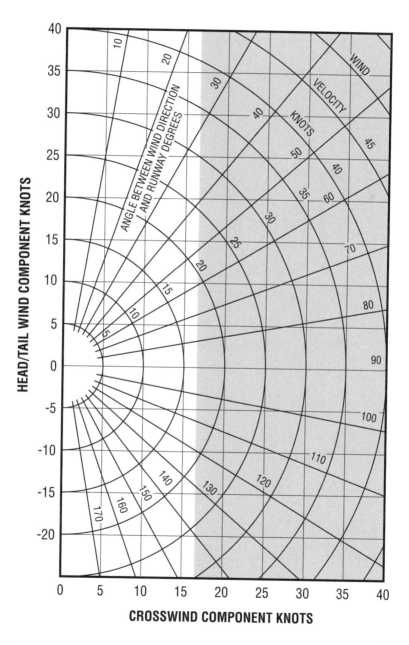

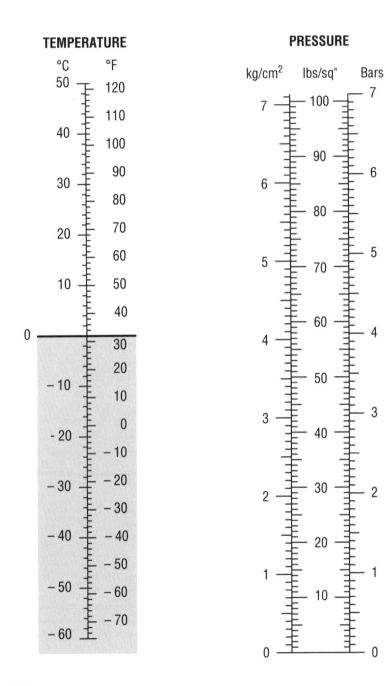

Distance-Metres/Feet

Metres	Feet
1	3·28
2	6·56
3	9·84
4	13·12
5	16·40
6	19·69
7	22·97
8	26·25
9	29·53
10	32·81
20	65·62
30	98·43
40	131·23
50	164·04
60	196·85
70	229·66
80	262·47
90	295·28
100	328·08
200	656·16
300	984·25
400	1,312·34
500	1,640·42
600	1,968·50
700	2,296·59
800	2,624·67
900	2,952·76
1000	3,280·84
2000	6,561·70
3000	9,842·50
4000	13,123·40
5000	16,404·20
6000	19,685·00
7000	22,965·90
8000	26,246·70
9000	29,527·60
10000	32,808·40

Feet	Metres
1	0·30
2	0·61
3	0·91
4	1·22
5	1·52
6	1·83
7	2·13
8	2·44
9	2·74
10	3·05
20	6·10
30	9·14
40	12·19
50	15·24
60	18·29
70	21·34
80	24·38
90	27·43
100	30·48
200	60·96
300	91·44
400	121·92
500	152·40
600	182·88
700	213·36
800	243·84
900	274·32
1000	304·80
2000	609·60
3000	914·40
4000	1,219·20
5000	1,524·00
6000	1,828·80
7000	2,133·60
8000	2,438·40
9000	2,743·20
10000	3,048·00

Conversion Factors:

Metres to Feet x 3.28084
Feet to Metres x 0.3048

Distance-KM/Nautical Miles/Statute Miles

NM	Km	St
1	1·85	1·15
2	3·70	2·30
3	5·56	3·45
4	7·41	4·60
5	9·26	5·75
6	11·11	6·90
7	12·96	8·06
8	14·82	9·21
9	16·67	10·36
10	18·52	11·51
20	37·04	23·02
30	55·56	34·52
40	74·08	46·03
50	92·60	57·54
60	111·12	69·05
70	129·64	80·55
80	148·16	92·06
90	166·68	103·57
100	185·2	115·1
200	370·4	230·2
300	555·6	345·2
400	740·8	460·3
500	926·0	575·4
600	1111·2	690·5
700	1296·4	805·6
800	1481·6	920·6
900	1666·8	1035·7

Km	NM	St
1	·54	·62
2	1·08	1·24
3	1·62	1·86
4	2·16	2·49
5	2·70	3·11
6	3·24	3·73
7	3·78	4·35
8	4·32	4·97
9	4·86	5·59
10	5·40	6·21
20	10·80	12·43
30	16·20	18·64
40	21·60	24·86
50	27·00	31·07
60	32·40	37·28
70	37·80	43·50
80	43·20	49·71
90	48·60	55·92
100	54·0	62·1
200	108·0	124·3
300	162·0	186·4
400	216·0	248·6
500	270·0	310·7
600	324·0	372·8
700	378·0	435·0
800	432·0	497·1
900	486·0	559·2

St	NM	Km
1	·87	1·61
2	1·74	3·22
3	2·61	4·83
4	3·48	6·44
5	4·34	8·05
6	5·21	9·66
7	6·08	11·27
8	6·95	12·87
9	7·82	14·48
10	8·69	16·09
20	17·38	32·19
30	26·07	48·28
40	34·76	64·37
50	43·45	80·47
60	52·14	96·56
70	60·83	112·65
80	69·52	128·75
90	78·21	144·84
100	86·9	161·0
200	173·8	321·9
300	260·7	482·8
400	347·6	643·7
500	434·5	804·7
600	521·4	965·6
700	608·3	1126·5
800	695·2	1287·5
900	782·1	1448·4

Conversion Factors:

Statute Miles to Nautical Miles x 0.868976
Statute Miles to Kilometres x 1.60934
Kilometres to Statute Miles x 0.62137
Kilometres to Nautical Miles x 0.539957
Nautical Miles to Statute Miles x 1.15078
Nautical Miles to Kilometres x 1.852

Weight

lbs	Kg	Kg	lbs
1	·45	1	2·20
2	·91	2	4·41
3	1·36	3	6·61
4	1·81	4	8·82
5	2·27	5	11·02
6	2·72	6	13·23
7	3·18	7	15·43
8	3·63	8	17·64
9	4·08	9	19·84
10	4·54	10	22·05
20	9·07	20	44·09
30	13·61	30	66·14
40	18·14	40	88·18
50	22·68	50	110·23
60	27·22	60	132·28
70	31·75	70	154·32
80	36·29	80	176·37
90	40·82	90	198·42
100	45·4	100	220·5
200	90·7	200	440·9
300	136·1	300	661·4
400	181·4	400	881·8
500	226·8	500	1102·3
600	272·2	600	1322·8
700	317·5	700	1543·2
800	362·9	800	1763·7
900	408·2	900	1984·2
1000	453·6	1000	2204·6
2000	907·2	2000	4409·2
3000	1360·8	3000	6613·9
4000	1814·4	4000	8818·5
5000	2268·0	5000	11023·1
6000	2721·5	6000	13227·7
7000	3175·1	7000	15432·3
8000	3628·7	8000	17637·0
9000	4082·3	9000	19841·6
10000	4535·9	10000	22046·2

Conversion Factors:

lbs to Kilograms x 0.45359
Kilograms to lbs x 2.20462

Volume (Fluid)

Litres	Imp. Gall	U.S. Gall	U.S. Gall	Imp. Gall	Litres	Imp. Gall	U.S. Gall	Litres
1	0.22	0.26	1	0.83	3.79	1	1.20	4.55
2	0.44	0.53	2	1.67	7.57	2	2.40	9.09
3	0.66	0.79	3	2.50	11.36	3	3.60	13.64
4	0.88	1.06	4	3.33	15.14	4	4.80	18.18
5	1.10	1.32	5	4.16	18.93	5	6.00	22.73
6	1.32	1.59	6	5.00	22.71	6	7.21	27.28
7	1.54	1.85	7	5.83	26.50	7	8.41	31.82
8	1.76	2.11	8	6.66	30.28	8	9.61	36.37
9	1.98	2.38	9	7.49	34.07	9	10.81	40.91
10	2.20	2.64	10	8.33	37.85	10	12.01	45.46
20	4.40	5.28	20	16.65	75.71	20	24.02	90.92
30	6.60	7.93	30	24.98	113.56	30	36.03	136.38
40	8.80	10.57	40	33.31	151.41	40	48.04	181.84
50	11.00	13.21	50	41.63	189.27	50	60.05	227.30
60	13.20	15.85	60	49.96	227.12	60	72.06	272.76
70	15.40	18.49	70	58.29	264.97	70	84.07	318.22
80	17.60	21.14	80	66.61	302.82	80	96.08	363.68
90	19.80	23.78	90	74.94	340.68	90	108.09	409.14
100	22.00	26.42	100	83.27	378.54	100	120.09	454.60
200	44.00	52.84						
300	66.00	79.26						
400	88.00	105.68						
500	110.00	132.10						
600	132.00	158.52						
700	154.00	184.94						
800	176.00	211.36						
900	198.00	237.78						
1000	220.00	264.20						

Conversion Factors:

Imperial Gallons to Litres x 4.54596
Litres to Imperial Gallons x 0.219975
U.S. Gallons to Litres x 3.78541
Litres to U.S. Gallons x 0.264179
Imperial Gallons to U.S. Gallons x 1.20095
U.S. Gallons to Imperial Gallons x 0.832674

R22—Index